Bathrooms

A Sunset Design Guide

by Bridget Biscotti Bradley and the editors of *Sunset*

Contents

Have you been living with a bathroom that doesn't fit your needs, the needs of your family, or your personal style? Now is the time to take action and create a space that feels like home to you. This book will guide you through all of your shopping choices—from inexpensive tile and paint to luxury spa amenities. You'll also find advice on materials and fixtures that are better for the environment and better for the indoor air quality of your home. Today it's easier than ever to make water conservation a top priority in your bathroom remodel.

Throughout the book you'll find words of wisdom from our panel of experts. Reading their advice and seeing how they solved problems for their clients in the case studies will inspire you to see the possibilities in your bathroom.

6

36

ISBN-13: 978-0-376-01444-3
ISBN-10: 0-376-01444-X
Library of Congress Control Number: 2012945699

Second Edition. First Printing 2013
Printed in the United States of America

OXMOOR HOUSE, INC.
Editorial Director: Leah McLaughlin
Creative Director: Felicity Keane
Brand Manager: Fonda Hitchcock
Managing Editor: Rebecca Benton

TIME HOME ENTERTAINMENT INC.
Publisher: Jim Childs
VP, Strategy & Business Development: Steven Sandonato
Executive Director, Marketing Services: Carol Pittard
Executive Director, Retail & Special Sales: Tom Misfud
Director, Bookazine Development and Marketing: Laura Adam
Executive Publishing Director: Joy Butts
Associate Publishing Director: Megan Pearlman
Finance Director: Glenn Buonocore
Associate General Counsel: Helen Wan

SUNSET PUBLISHING
President: Barb Newton
VP, Editor-in-Chief: Kitty Morgan

CONTRIBUTORS TO THIS BOOK

Managing Editor: Bridget Biscotti Bradley
Photo Editor: Philippine Scali
Production Manager: Linda M. Bouchard
Photo Coordinator: Danielle Johnson
Editorial Assistant: Holly Durocher
Imaging Specialist: Kimberley Navabpour
Project Editor: Sarah Doss
Proofreader: John Edmonds
Indexer: Marjorie Joy
Series Designer: Vasken Guiragossian

To order additional publications, call 1-800-765-6400
For more books to enrich your life, visit **oxmoorhouse.com**

Visit Sunset online at **sunset.com**

For the most comprehensive selection of Sunset books, visit **sunsetbooks.com**

For more exciting home and garden ideas, visit **myhomeideas.com**

Design Panel

The following design and building professionals from across the United States lent their enormous talent and valuable advice to the pages of this book.

Beth Wells Gensemer
ARCHITECT

Beth Wells Gensemer Architecture, LLC, is a Los Angeles firm that specializes in residential construction and remodeling. Beth earned a Master of Architecture from the University of Pennsylvania and is a licensed architect in the states of California and New York. She is a member of the American Institute of Architects and is LEED accredited.
www.bwg-a.com | *Beth shows us a clean and modern bathroom design on pages 62–63.*

Heidi Pribell
INTERIOR DESIGNER

Heidi Pribell Interiors was founded in 1996 in Cambridge, Massachusetts, and creates evocative, inspired environments. Heidi graduated from Harvard University and the New York School of Interior Design and has been a dealer of fine arts and antiques. Her work blends a modern, contemporary aesthetic with a passion for culture and the history of fine design and decoration.
www.heidipribell.com | *See how Heidi creates unique patterns with tile on pages 64–65.*

Dennis Fox
ARCHITECT

Dennis Fox, principal of Fox Design Group, earned his Bachelor and Master of Architecture degrees at the University of California, Berkeley,

and is a licensed architect in the state of California. Dennis has extensive experience designing remodels and additions that improve the space use, circulation, and lighting in existing homes.
www.foxdesigngroup.com | *See Dennis's sun-drenched spa bath on pages 120–123.*

Lou Ann Bauer
INTERIOR DESIGNER

Lou Ann Bauer, ASID, is a graduate of U. C. Berkeley with a BA in fine arts, and a BS in interior design from San Jose State University in California. She is the principal of her own firm in San Francisco, Bauer Interior Design. Lou Ann has combined her art training with the function of interior design to create a whimsical and colorful mix of furnishings and environments. She also owns a charming San Francisco knob and pull retail store called Bauerware (www.bauerware.com).
www.bauerdesign.com | *See a bath that Lou Ann designed around cabinet hardware on pages 200–201.*

Anne Laird-Blanton
ARCHITECT

Anne Laird-Blanton, AIA, was born and raised in the South, was educated at the University of Tennessee, and holds architectural licenses in New York and California. Anne combines a love for architecture and a concern for her clients' needs with a practical knowledge of building codes, requirements, and the approval process. She is actively involved with the American Institute of Architects and served as secretary of the California Council (AIACC) from 2003 to 2004 and as the 2006 president of AIA San Francisco. **www.albdesigns.com** | *See Anne's bright and airy master bath on pages 174–177.*

David Gast
ARCHITECT

David S. Gast and Associates is a service-oriented architectural practice that was founded in San Francisco in 1980. David received a bachelor of arts in architecture from Stanford University and is a licensed architect in the states of California and Hawaii. His firm specializes in custom residential projects, both renovations and new construction, and in moderate-scale commercial and educational buildings.

www.gastarchitects.com | *David shows us a small bathroom that's big on storage on pages 94–95, and a stylish master bath on pages 202–203.*

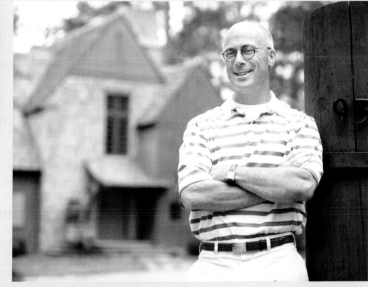

Bill Ingram
ARCHITECT

After graduating from Auburn University with a degree in architecture in 1983, Bill Ingram settled in Birmingham, where he runs a private firm designing houses throughout the Southeast, as well as around the country. His work has been featured in *Southern Accents, House and Garden, Veranda, House Beautiful,* and *Cottage Living.* **www.billingramarchitect.com** | *Bill show-cases his Southern style in a bathroom on pages 178–179.*

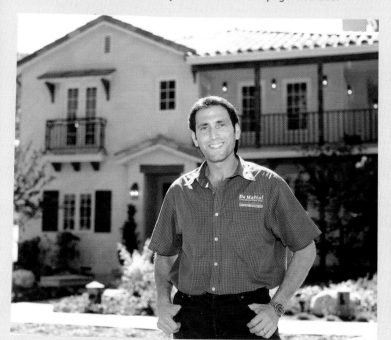

Kathryn Rogers
ARCHITECT

Kathryn A. Rogers is the principal architect and founder of Sogno Design Group, which focuses on residential design in the San Francisco Bay Area. She received her bachelor of architecture at Virginia Polytechnic and has a background in historic preservation and restoration. She was a board member of Architects, Designers, and Planners for Social Responsibility (ADPSR) for 10 years in Washington, D.C., and the East Bay and continues to find ways to incorporate green building methods in her projects. **www.sognodesigngroup.com** | *See Kathryn's eco-friendly bathroom remodel on pages 92–93, and a master bath addition on pages 148–149.*

Mark De Mattei
BUILDER

Mark De Mattei formed De Mattei Construction in 1985 as one of the commercial builders helping to lead the revitalization of downtown San Jose, California, and its landmark buildings. In the 1990s, the firm shifted its focus to residential remodeling and custom homebuilding. Today, De Mattei Construction has built or remodeled more than 1,000 homes. The company ranks among the largest residential remodelers in the U.S. **www.demattei.com** | *See Mark's take on a bathroom that's pure luxury on pages 150–151.*

Terrell Goeke
INTERIOR DESIGNER

Terrell Goeke, a licensed interior designer for 27 years with a BA in interior design, specializes in residential interior architecture and design for kitchens and bathrooms. He owns and operates a retail store, Terrell Goeke, in Chicago's Merchandise Mart and a custom cabinet shop that is a certified manufacturer of eco-friendly wood cabinets. **www.terrellgoeke.com** | *Learn more about Terrell's eco-friendly cabinets on pages 72–73.*

Chapter 1

Getting Started

So you've made the decision to renovate your bathroom—
congratulations! Once you're through, you'll wonder how you ever
got by with the old one. Before you start making decisions on
materials, colors, and fixtures, look over the selection of bathrooms
we've assembled in the following pages to gently ease into the
remodeling waters. As you start to imagine your new bathroom,
consider how many elements need to be improved, as well as
possible new layouts that will make the space perform better.

Hexagonal wall tiles, pale floral wallpaper, and soft roman shades add color and texture to this feminine, vintage-inspired bathroom.

Bathroom Considerations

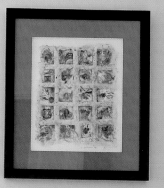

The owners of this small guest bath decided to splurge on basket-weave glass tiles for the floor, making it an unforgettable room in the house.

Which bathroom you're remodeling will dictate what's at the top of your shopping list. If it's a half bath, you might be looking for lighting fixtures and a wall finish that will make it look like more of an extension of the adjoining living area. If it's a bath used mostly by children, nonslip flooring, clever storage solutions, and materials that can take a beating are your main priorities. The following pages show a variety of options and discuss the different needs for master baths, spa baths, shared baths, kids' baths, and half baths.

LEFT Easy-to-care-for materials—such as glazed ceramic floor tiles, a porcelain console sink, and painted walls—are great choices for downstairs bathrooms that get a lot of use. This example shows how stunning simplicity can be.

TOP RIGHT Half baths are the best places to use materials that won't stand up well to moisture, such as this textural grass-cloth wallpaper made from real plant fibers. The frosted glass mirror frame was placed over a series of blocks while being fired to give it this pattern.

BOTTOM RIGHT Situated off a girl's bedroom, this bath uses the same window treatments and color scheme, giving the two spaces a cohesive look. Feminine light fixtures and a floral-patterned window seat cushion personalize the space.

Usually located near living areas on the first floor, half baths (also called powder rooms) have a toilet and sink but no shower or tub. They are quite often small, borrowing space from under the stairs or a hall closet. Having a half bath near a living area is a true luxury, as guests don't have to wander into more private areas of a home to use a shared bathroom and you don't have to keep that shared bathroom spotless just in case someone drops by unannounced. While its small size can make it difficult to squeeze everything you'd like into a half bath, the upside of the minimal amount of square footage is that you'll be able to afford higher-priced materials and fixtures.

With no tub or shower, you can use materials that might otherwise require a good deal of maintenance when subjected to daily steam and splashes. However, if you don't already have a bathroom fan, take this opportunity to install one. There's still some steam that can come from the sink, plus the noise creates privacy and the fan helps remove odor, a good idea for half baths that open onto living spaces or kitchens.

TOP Half baths are ideal places to hang a fine art collection, as there is no steam from a bath or shower to harm it.

BOTTOM The same distressed wood paneling in the hallway was used to construct the small cabinet in this half bath to create a seamless transition when the door is open.

OPPOSITE PAGE A starburst mirror and mirrored vanity reflect light from the adjoining living space, making a small powder room feel larger.

INTERIOR DESIGNER
HEIDI PRIBELL ON

Designing Half Baths

Half baths have the same level of importance as an entrance foyer because they make a statement to your guests. "I'll come up with a concept that the client identifies with, be it a location or a culture, and design around that. It's a great opportunity to use wallpapers and wood paneling to beef up the interior architecture. I also like to convert smaller pieces of furniture into vanities for half baths."

OPPOSITE PAGE, TOP LEFT Iridescent glass mosaic tiles can put a strain on a bathroom budget, but in a half bath the low square footage works in your favor.

OPPOSITE PAGE, TOP RIGHT Several shades of lavender and Moroccan accessories transformed this plain and narrow bathroom into something special.

OPPOSITE PAGE, BOTTOM LEFT In this quirky upstairs guest bath, a vintage side table was repurposed into a vanity.

OPPOSITE PAGE, BOTTOM RIGHT Narrow stone tiles have an architectural weight to them that works well with the concrete countertop on this small, wall-mounted vanity.

RIGHT Multicolor slate tiles and a cheery yellow wall create a casual, open feeling in this hall bath.

Shared Baths

During the morning rush, it's helpful to have two sinks and a shower with a privacy wall on the bottom half so the whole family can get ready at once.

When there's only one full bathroom in a house, it's usually a high-traffic area that needs to function well for people of all ages. Choose materials and fixtures that can handle constant use. If more than one person tends to use the bathroom at the same time, try to find room for an extra sink. A vanity with two sinks will give you the most storage, but in small bathrooms, two pedestal or wall-hung sinks will make the room seem larger. You can always add shelves, hooks, or freestanding furniture for additional storage. If you run out of wall space for towel bars, install hooks for towels on the back of the door.

The level of privacy desired by multiple users in a shared bathroom varies widely, both from each other and from the outside world through windows. When architect David Gast designs a shared bath, he asks the family a series of questions to determine the "level of psychological and physical separation" needed to make them comfortable. One way to add privacy is to utilize an opaque shower curtain or install frosted

A sunny shared bath, built with inexpensive materials, blends seamlessly into this 1940s house. White ceramic floor tiles with black diamond dots are carried through from the adjoining hallway. Old dressers were given a fresh coat of paint and ceramic tile tops, and there are plenty of open shelves and towel racks for the whole family. Golden walls warm up the space.

glass doors so that one person can take a shower while another is using the vanity. Putting the toilet in a separate room with a door is ideal if you have the space. Otherwise, you can build a dividing wall between the toilet and the tub or sink for the illusion of privacy.

Most shared baths are situated between two bedrooms and, ideally, allow access from each one. If you're doing a full remodel and removing the existing drywall, add extra insulation between the studs so that people sleeping in the adjacent rooms won't be bothered by running water or flushing toilets.

TOP LEFT An antique dresser finds new life as a double vanity with above-counter sinks. Separate mirrors and a wall organizer with hooks for towels and toiletries make the space more functional for multiple users.

BOTTOM LEFT Open shelves with baskets keep toiletries visible yet organized. Assign each bathroom user his or her own container. Wall hooks keep jewelry untangled and ready to wear.

RIGHT A desk with a hutch for storage separates two vanity areas—one for kids and one for adults.

Kids' Baths

Step stools make it easier to reach the trough sink for teeth brushing or boat racing. Kids love oversized showerheads that make getting clean feel like playing in a rainstorm.

Creating a bathroom that meets the needs of small children is a great choice for young families. Picking a theme, like sea animals or sailboats, or adding bright colors and whimsical accessories is the fun part, but the main concerns should be safety and materials that are durable and easy to keep clean.

Beyond standard safety measures that you would implement whether you're remodeling or not—installing safety latches on cabinet doors, putting childproof covers on receptacles, and installing a toilet lid lock—there are many ways to make a bathroom more kid-friendly. Choose slip-resistant flooring, make sure there are no sharp edges on counters or partition walls, buy a bathtub with a textured surface on the bottom (or use textured floor mats with the existing tub), and install scald-free tub and shower valves (see page 147).

One of the biggest issues for kids in the bathroom is that standard heights and clearances (see pages 34–35) don't work for them. You can avoid the need for step stools by lowering all or part of a vanity so small children can reach the sink, but you may eventually need to replace the cabinets if you customize them in this way (see page 20). Some toilet manufacturers make shorter versions of standard toilets, which can be replaced easily later on. Include open storage options kids can reach, such as cubbies on the floor or sand pails hung low on the wall, to encourage them to put away bath toys.

LEFT If it makes more sense to keep the surfaces neutral, you can still liven up a kids' bath with whimsical accessories such as cabinet pulls, mirrors, and storage containers.

ABOVE A trip to a tile manufacturer's "seconds" yard may not yield enough of one style to cover an entire shower, but it provides an opportunity for a creative patchwork design in a kids' bathroom.

LEFT The handheld showerhead was mounted low on the wall so that kids can reach it. Glass fish-shaped tiles and the towel bar were also installed around eye-level.

RIGHT A combination of lavender, white, and gray make this teenage girl's bathroom sophisticated enough to transition into a guest bath when she leaves home. Hexagonal mosaic marble floor tiles give it an upscale look.

OPPOSITE PAGE, TOP Architect Kathryn Rogers found unique ways to add storage in this small bath. Behind the door is a recessed cabinet that's just a few inches deep but can hold makeup, nail polish, and toiletries.

OPPOSITE PAGE, BOTTOM This custom cabinet provides plenty of room for all the things a teenage girl needs, including a handy spot to keep the curling iron where it won't clutter the lavender CaesarStone countertop.

INTERIOR DESIGNER
TERRELL GOEKE ON

Kid-Friendly Vanities

Instead of lowering the vanity so kids can reach, keep it at the standard height and incorporate a stool in the toe kick (right) that can be pulled out when needed so you aren't constantly tripping over it. "If the family really wants a lower vanity, I suggest doing a split-height vanity at 33 or 34 inches high—a little lower than average so that adults have to stoop a bit and kids have to reach a bit for a happy medium."

Master Baths

The master bathroom is your own private oasis, where you can shut the door and hide from the kids while relaxing in a hot bath after an exhausting day. Used by one person or a couple, master baths often have space for a separate shower and bathtub area, as well as a small room with a door for the toilet. You don't have to take the needs of children into account, so you can choose materials and finishes that require a little extra care.

If you share a master bath with another person and have only one sink, now is the time to think about adding a second one so you can both brush your teeth without taking turns for spitting. When there's no room for a second sink, consider adding a large mirror so that two people can more easily use the vanity area at the same time.

LEFT This cottage-style master bath has wide-plank pine floors and wainscot around a half wall that hides the toilet area from view.

RIGHT For people who prefer easy-to-maintain materials, porcelain floor tile looks like stone but is practically indestructible.

BELOW Located off a wraparound porch, this master bath invites you to enjoy your morning cup of coffee outdoors while lounging in your robe before getting ready for the day.

Extremely large master baths can incorporate special features, such as walk-in closets and dressing areas. If you're dreaming of a larger space, look into the possibility of extending the master bath into an adjoining closet or bedroom.

ARCHITECT
BILL INGRAM ON

Creating Separate Spaces

Couples generally share a master bath, where each person needs a little of his or her own space. "Sometimes I'll design separate bathrooms off a master bedroom, but in old houses where you don't have space for that, a shared master bath can work if you give people some of their own territory by zoning different areas of the room so there's both privacy and interconnection."

OPPOSITE PAGE
A two-sided vanity provides plenty of counter space and storage for each user. The height of the vanity blocks a direct view of the glass-enclosed shower area from the entrance, while sunlight from the windows bouncing off the mirrors keeps the back of the room bright.

Decorated much like a living room, with a collection of plates on the wall and a comfortable slipcovered armchair next to a glass-topped table for books, this is a master bath to enjoy at any time of day. A raised whirlpool tub sits in the corner, and muslin curtains hide toiletries under a double vanity with a wooden countertop.

Spa Baths

Inspired by a hotel in Bali, this spa bathroom features a soaking tub and large windows that bring in the outdoors.

If you have the budget to be indulgent, turn your master bathroom into a home spa by installing a luxury bath or steam shower. "More people are traveling and getting to experience all these great hotel spas, and they're coming back home thinking about incorporating similar features into their own bathrooms," says architect Anne Laird-Blanton.

Most floors, even those in older homes, can handle the weight of a standard tub because the water is spread across a relatively large surface. But when you get into carved stone tubs, or deep and narrow tubs, you'll want to make sure the floor can handle the weight. Also consider how you'll get these large and heavy tubs into the bathroom, which can be a big challenge when it's not located on the first floor.

Whirlpool baths use a pump to recirculate warm water while jets massage your back and legs. Some models offer chromatherapy, which turns the water different colors to promote healing and balance your energy. If being blasted by water jets isn't your idea of relaxation, look at an air bath, which has tiny holes along the base of the tub. It can bubble gently like champagne, or with more vigor for a light or medium massage. Not into bubbles at all? Your relaxation might come in the form of a soaking tub. These deep tubs allow the water to come up to your shoulders—some even include a reservoir for spillover.

Install speakers on either side of the bathroom so you can listen to relaxing music, and put a dimmer switch on the lights. Finish off your spa bathroom with earth tones, natural materials such as plants and stone, and a do-not-disturb sign for the door.

ABOVE Dimming the lights creates a soft glow in this spa bath, and the dark wood finishes help keep the space tranquil. A large sliding door opens onto a private courtyard.

LEFT Decorated with pink roses plucked from the garden beyond, the edge of this round tub encourages harmony with nature.

ABOVE Architect Beth Gensemer designed this monochromatic spa bath to have a light, open feeling in a modern-style home. The owners can listen to music while soaking in the tub under a large open window.

RIGHT An oversized custom tub with views of a private garden make this a popular spot for kids and adults alike.

OPPOSITE PAGE A soaking tub with a reservoir around it allows you to bring the water to chin level, which helps relieve the tension in your neck and shoulders.

Questions to Ask

The more hours you spend evaluating your current bathroom and planning for the new one, the more likely it is that you'll end up with something spectacular.

Before you start shopping for new materials or meeting with professionals to discuss your renovation plans (see Chapter 8), spend some time thinking about your current bathroom setup. Considering its strengths and weaknesses will lead you to some decisions about what changes need to be made and what's working as is.

It's tempting to focus immediately on the way you want your new bathroom to look, but bathrooms also need to function effectively. Depending on how the bathroom is used, you may want to change the layout of the room in addition to updating fixtures and finishes. Answering the following questions will help you decide how extensive a remodel you may need to undertake.

- What's your main reason for wanting to remodel your bathroom?

- How many people will be using the room on a regular basis? Are any of those people of above-average or below-average height? Will the bathroom be used by an elderly or disabled person?

- Do you like compartmentalized layouts or a more open look? Will more than one person use the room at the same time?

- How's the traffic flow? Is there adequate clearance between fixtures? Can existing doors and windows be relocated to improve traffic patterns, if necessary?

- What secondary activity areas would you like to include—dressing area, makeup table, or exercise or laundry facilities?

- Are you planning any structural changes, such as a greenhouse window or an addition to the room? Is there a full basement, crawl space, or concrete slab beneath the bathroom? Is the floor strong enough for any heavy new fixtures you want to include?

- What kind of water supply pipes do you have (i.e., galvanized or copper)? How's your water pressure? Do any pipes leak? Have you had a high number of clogs or backups?

- Do you want to add any new fixtures? Is the toilet where you want it? Is the showerhead at a convenient height? Are fixtures and fittings easy to clean? Do they waste water or energy?

- Is your current bathroom safe? Are surfaces slippery? Is the tub easy to get into and out of? Are all electrical circuits protected by ground-fault circuit interrupters (GFCIs)?

- What type of heating system do you have? Is it adequate? Do you want to add a radiant heat system in the floor or extend a forced-air system into the bathroom?

- How's the climate in your bathroom after a steamy shower? If ventilation is a problem, is there a way to supplement it with operable windows or skylights, or do you need to upgrade your electrical ventilation system?

- What's the amp rating of your electrical service? Do you ever blow a fuse when using electrical equipment, such as a hair dryer, in the bathroom? Will any new fixtures require you to add electrical circuits?

- Do you need to improve upon the existing lighting plan? What natural light sources are possible?

- Evaluate your bathroom's surfaces. Are any of them damaged or dated?

- What are your bathroom storage requirements? Do you prefer open storage and display, or closed cabinets and closets?

- Are you willing or able to do any or all of the demolition or building yourself?

- How long do you have to complete the project?

- What budget figure do you have in mind?

Creating a Layout

A small room can make the layout more challenging in some ways yet easier than a large, open room in that you likely have fewer configuration options.

Creating an accurate drawing of your current bathroom will be an invaluable tool as you begin to plan for your remodel. This sketch will also help you communicate with design professionals and showroom personnel.

Start by sketching your present layout on a piece of paper, without worrying about scale. Include rough locations for windows and doors, plumbing fixtures, and lighting. Then use a tape measure to measure the dimensions of each wall. Start at countertop height in one corner and measure across to the other corner. Continue around the room, including separate measurements for doors and windows. Then measure the floor-to-ceiling height of each wall. The measurements for facing walls should match—if not, something is out of square.

Once you've got your measurements, draw a base map to scale using graph paper, a ruler, and a pencil. Or you may prefer to draw it on the computer using a graphics application. There are also home remodeling software programs that will insert the correct architectural symbols on your drawing, which is helpful if you plan to submit the base map for a building permit.

BASE MAP

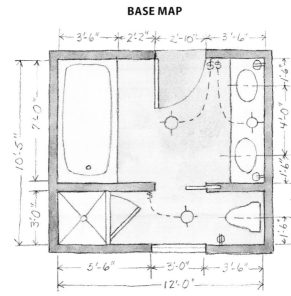

ARCHITECTURAL SYMBOLS

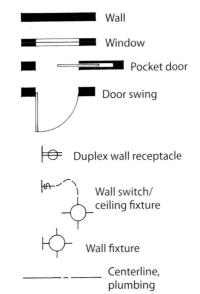

Wall

Window

Pocket door

Door swing

Duplex wall receptacle

Wall switch/
ceiling fixture

Wall fixture

Centerline,
plumbing

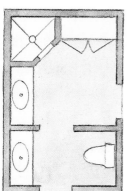

LEFT This 8-by-12-foot family bath has two points of entry. One person can close two doors to take a shower, and a second person can enter from another doorway to use the toilet area while the shower is in use.

RIGHT This 8-by-12-foot children's bath layout is great when multiple kids need to get ready for school at the same time. There are two points of entry leading to small areas that contain a sink and a toilet. In the center of the bathroom are a closet and a tub. Three kids can use the bathroom in privacy at the same time.

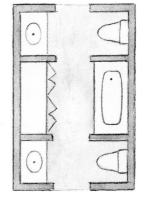

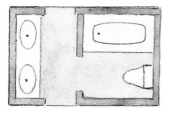

LEFT This 6-by-10-foot children's bath layout shows a smaller space that is still able to accommodate several users at once. Two or more kids can use the double vanity, while another can close the door to use the toilet or tub.

BELOW When you have a large space to work with, you can add extra amenities to the bathroom, such as an exercise area and walk-in closets.

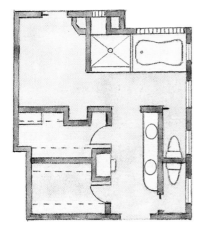

The sample base map shown at top right includes centerlines to sink plumbing and electrical symbols for receptacles, switches, and fixtures. Include these in your plan to show where wiring and plumbing currently exist, and then make several photocopies of your base map (if you hand-drew it) before drawing in existing elements such as the sink, toilet, shower, and tub.

Once you've got the base map finished, you can start experimenting with new layouts. The photos throughout this book will give you plenty of ideas. If you are working with a small space, you might have only one choice for where the toilet and tub can go. Larger spaces give you the opportunity to compartmentalize areas for multiple users.

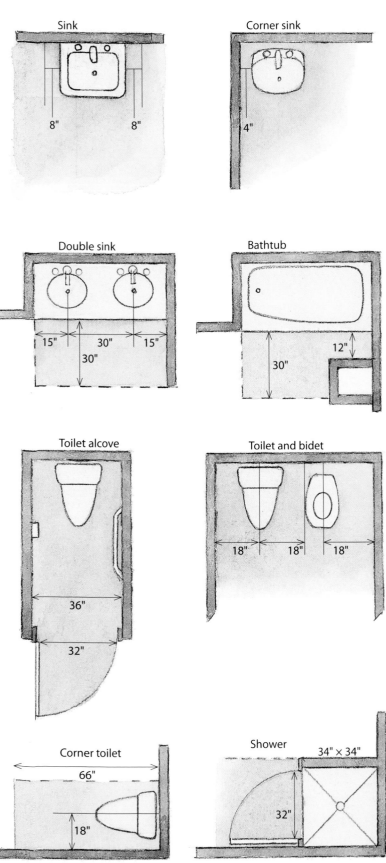

Sink

8"   8"

Corner sink

4"

Double sink

15"   30"   15"
30"

Bathtub

12"
30"

Toilet alcove

36"
32"

Toilet and bidet

18"   18"   18"

Corner toilet

66"
18"

Shower

34" × 34"
32"

Arranging Fixtures

There are many factors to consider when you're deciding where to place the sink, toilet, tub, and shower. Beyond where these fixtures will work best for the layout you have in mind, you need to pay attention to where current drains and water supply lines are. Installing a sink within a few inches of where the old one was or adding a second sink will require only minor plumbing changes. But moving the sink to the other side of the room will be more costly, as will moving a toilet, shower, or tub.

Keep in mind, however, that you will most likely remodel this bathroom only once. Architect Dennis Fox advises that you take this opportunity to make things the way you want them. "If we're taking an existing bathroom down to the studs and the homeowner wants to save a little money by leaving the toilet in the same location rather than rerouting the plumbing, my advice is if you're going this far, take everything apart and do it right," he says.

If you're adding on to your house or building a new bathroom, you can save a little money by having the new bathroom share a wall with an existing kitchen or bath so that you can tap into those supply and drain pipes rather than having to run new ones.

Heights and Clearances

Working with your base plan, position the largest unit (usually the bathtub or shower) first. Then place the sink or sinks where they are out of the traffic pattern, if possible, and allow ample elbowroom on each side. The toilet should be as far from the door as possible. If you are adding a bidet, it should be next to the toilet.

Building codes and industry guidelines specify certain clearances between, beside, and in front of bathroom fixtures to allow enough room for use, cleaning, and repair. The illustrations at left show general guidelines for clearances, but always check with your local building department, as rules can vary.

There are guidelines that specify standard heights for cabinets and countertops, showerheads and valves, and other accessories. You may want to customize heights if there are people of above- or below-average height using the bathroom, but keep in mind that you will have to work within the building code to pass your building inspection, plus the next homeowners may prefer to have standard heights for their countertops or wall-hung toilets. Drawing an elevation plan for one or two walls, like the one shown on the opposite page, will help you determine whether the spacing between a vanity and mirror will work, and exactly how much tile you need to order for tub surrounds or backsplashes.

The Final Plan

Draw scale outlines of the fixtures and cabinets you're considering and cut them out so you can move each one around on your base map and try different layouts. If you opted to draw your base plan on a computer, this is a much easier process. Home remodeling software programs often have pre-drawn cabinets and fixtures that you can customize with your dimensions. Some can also do a 3-D "walk through" of the room to help you visualize the space. Use your finished plan to reference throughout the remodeling process. You may also use it to apply for a building permit.

Having the right amount of space around each fixture, as well as materials and patterns that look great together, is the result of careful planning.

RECOMMENDED HEIGHTS

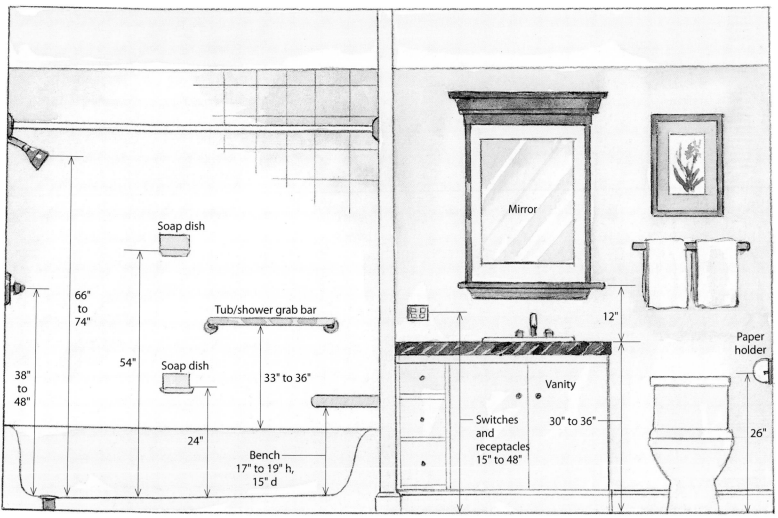

Soap dish

66" to 74"

Tub/shower grab bar

54"

Soap dish

38" to 48"

33" to 36"

24"

Bench 17" to 19" h, 15" d

Mirror

12"

Switches and receptacles 15" to 48"

Vanity

30" to 36"

Paper holder

26"

Chapter 2

Floors and Walls

In this chapter, we'll focus on the overall palette of the bathroom—the floors and walls. Because they are the largest surfaces in the room, how you decide to paint, tile, or otherwise cover them will have a big impact on the design and functionality of the space. To narrow down your options, focus on a color scheme and then choose the materials based on the level of maintenance that you can live with. As you wade through the choices, keep in mind the type of bathroom and how much use it will get.

Gleaming 12-inch terrazzo tiles reflect the geometric pattern of the ceramic tile wall.

Flooring Choices

Ceramic tiles installed in the bathroom that are larger than 4 by 4 inches should have a slightly textured surface to make them less slippery when wet.

The bathroom floor can make a statement of its own with bright colors and patterns, or it can be a neutral backdrop that allows other features to shine. However it serves the design of your bathroom, the flooring should also be slip resistant and able to withstand whatever level of abuse you or your kids might throw at it.

Ceramic, Porcelain, and Glass Tiles

Durable and naturally water resistant, ceramic and porcelain tiles are popular choices for the bathroom floor. You can find ceramic tiles in an incredible number of sizes, shapes, colors, and finishes—although not all ceramic tiles are rated as strong enough for floor use, so ask before you buy. Porcelain tiles are fired at a much higher temperature than ceramic, so they will always be strong enough for the floor. They also come in a wide variety of colors and sizes, and some manufacturers make porcelain tiles that are dead ringers for natural stone.

Using machine-made tiles in standard sizes is a great way to keep the cost of your remodel down. Play with various patterns, such as checkerboard or diagonal. Consider adding more expensive tiles that are perhaps handmade or have a decorative finish as accent pieces throughout the pattern.

Glossy tiles are slippery unless you're using them as mosaics, which will require enough grout to keep you on your feet. When you want to keep grout to a minimum, look for large ceramic or porcelain tiles with a bit of a texture on the surface to help with slip resistance. No matter how narrow or few your grout lines are, you'll need to keep them sealed to avoid stains down the line.

Glass tiles are usually installed on the walls, but you can find ones with a slightly textured or sanded surface that make them less slippery underfoot. Not all glass tiles are rated for floor use, but the ones that are will give your bathroom floor an unusual and beautiful look.

ABOVE Glass floor tiles in a random pattern tie the vanity and thick glass shower surround together.

RIGHT These rectangular and square ceramic tiles set in a basket-weave pattern prove you can get a unique high-end look without using stone. Matching tiles used around the base of the tub lead to cream-colored subway tiles topped with cap pieces.

BELOW Square porcelain floor tiles mimic slate in this bathroom but are far more durable.

INTERIOR DESIGNER
LOU ANN BAUER ON

Porcelain Tile

Natural stone tends not to wear well on a bathroom floor. "I steer clients who are less prone to maintain a stone floor toward porcelain tile instead of stone. Porcelain tiles are rugged, they have color throughout so you can miter an edge, and some look just like natural stone."

Stone

Natural stone is a high-end choice seen mostly in bathrooms that don't get a lot of abuse, such as master baths, spa baths, and half baths. There are many varieties to choose from, including granite, marble, limestone, travertine, slate, soapstone, and quartzite. Along with price, color, and durability, consider where the stone is quarried as part of your decision. It's more eco-friendly to select a stone that is quarried close to home than to have one shipped from halfway around the world.

Stone has become more popular in recent years because of radiant-heat mats that can be easily and inexpensively installed under the finished floor. Some people used to shy away from stone because it is cold underfoot, but they consider it now that it can be kept at a stable and warm temperature. Builder Mark De Mattei has seen some stone floors with a high iron content take on a yellowish hue after being heated repeatedly in a wet environment, so be sure to ask your stone dealer if

the type you're buying will work with radiant heat.

Be aware that the stone delivered to your house may not have the same color or veining as the sample you saw in the store. Natural stone is made in the earth, so there will be variations from slab to slab. If you're buying stone tile from a store that has it in stock, you might be able to look through boxes and pick the ones that fall within the color range you prefer. Otherwise, be sure to purchase at least 20 percent more than

you need so you can avoid pieces that are wildly different. Sometimes, however, the variety is what you're after, such as with multicolored slate, whose pieces can range from dark gray to bright reds and golds.

Stone can be smooth, tumbled, textured, glossy, or honed (matte). As with ceramic tiles, you want to avoid using large, glossy stone in wet areas because it will be slippery. Some types of stone are more susceptible to scratches and stains than others. Ask if the variety

you're interested in comes presealed and if it needs to be resealed on a regular basis. Most do.

Your contractor should be able to advise you on whether your existing floor is strong enough to support the weight of stone. If you are installing it yourself, walk across the floor and see if you can detect any soft or bouncy areas. These will need to be repaired before you install any tile—especially stone, as grout and even the stone itself can crack if it is not on a stable surface.

OPPOSITE PAGE, LEFT Large limestone tiles wrap around the border of this bathroom, while slender rectangular tiles run in bands with mosaics between each one, creating a rug effect in the center of the room.

OPPOSITE PAGE, RIGHT Travertine floor tiles with chiseled edges have a textured surface that makes them slip resistant.

ABOVE LEFT Smooth stones attached to mesh backings install just like mosaic tile and lend a distinctively earthy feel to this bathroom. On a shower floor, they give a nice massage to bare feet.

ABOVE RIGHT A smooth gray and white marble floor is broken up by strips of green stone mosaic tiles. A greenish-gray ceiling blends the colors together.

TOP These concrete tiles lend an old-world feel to a new bathroom.

MIDDLE Plain concrete sprinkled with dry pigment while still wet results in a mottled appearance. Install a hydronic heat system before installing so your feet stay warm as you step out of the bathtub.

BOTTOM Terrazzo tiles have a strong pattern and can incorporate practically any color you'd like with glass or stone. This example uses pieces of olive and aqua glass.

OPPOSITE PAGE Caramel-colored carbonized bamboo flooring looks right at home in this nature-inspired design featuring olive green glass wall tiles and a row of bamboo plants in white pots on the shower ledge.

Concrete

Not all concrete is gray and industrial looking. Concrete is an incredibly versatile material that can be left in its natural state or colored and textured to mimic stone, porcelain, or ceramic. The surface may be polished smooth or made slip resistant with small stones (called aggregate) incorporated in the mix. An installer can also cut shallow grooves that mimic grout lines in a poured concrete floor, making it look more like tiles. Real concrete tiles, which have been used around the world for decades, are making a comeback. Concrete tiles are less expensive to install than a poured concrete floor and are available in patterns and colors to suit any style of bathroom.

If you're removing the existing floor or building a new bathroom, consider pouring a new concrete subfloor and giving it a decorative finish. You can also pour a thin concrete topping over an existing subfloor. Just because you can buy a bag of concrete for a few bucks to hold up your fence post, don't assume that a concrete floor will be inexpensive. Not only do installers use a different kind of concrete for interiors, but the finishing process is labor intensive, so concrete can end up costing as much as high-end stone or glass.

As with tile and some stones, you can install a radiant-heat system underneath the finished floor so that the concrete isn't so cold to walk on. Seal regularly to prevent staining.

Terrazzo

Traditionally poured onsite, terrazzo is a concrete floor with aggregate that is troweled and polished to reveal its colorful embedded pieces. While you could have a terrazzo floor poured in your bathroom, a less expensive option is to use the material in tile form made with a resin binder that won't need to be resealed, or a concrete binder that will. Many manufacturers use recycled stone, glass, and porcelain in their terrazzo tiles, making this an eco-friendly choice as well.

Bamboo

Bamboo flooring is sometimes mistaken for wood, but bamboo is actually a grass that can be harvested every three to five years, making it a rapidly renewable and therefore green building material. The stalks are dried, pressed, and laminated into solid boards that are then cut into planks of various lengths and widths. Like wood, bamboo does expand and contract as moisture conditions change, although vertical-grain patterns are more stable than those with horizontal grain. Once limited to blond or carbonized colors, bamboo is now available in a range of hues. For bathroom use, it's wise to seal the floor after installation to avoid water damage, even if you buy factory-finished planks.

Wood

It may not be the most practical choice, but in some bathrooms wood just works. Wood is warm underfoot and has a classic, homey look, but whether it's hardwood planks or factory-finished engineered flooring, wood can be damaged by moisture. It can also expand and contract as the room fluctuates from wet and warm to dry and cold, resulting in cracks and splitting.

If you want wood in your bathroom, prefinished engineered wood and reclaimed wood will fare a little better because they are more dimensionally stable. Keep the wood well sealed, mop up any spills immediately, and install an efficient bathroom fan so the wood stays as dry as possible, and it may last a long time.

There are a wide variety of wood species and sizes available in both solid wood and engineered wood flooring, from sleek Brazilian cherry to wide-plank pine with a distressed finish. If you are concerned about deforestation and fair trade, buy wood that has been certified by the Forest Stewardship Council (FSC), as that will ensure the product comes from responsibly managed forests.

While most wood flooring is nailed into a wood subfloor, you can buy floating engineered wood floor planks if your bathroom has a concrete subfloor, or glue down solid wood planks. For people who love the aesthetic of wood but find it too impractical in the bathroom, there are porcelain tiles in plank sizes that will give you the look of a wood floor, if not the feel.

LEFT Teak wood floors naturally have a burnt orange hue. Their warm color complements the grayish blue glass tiles in this bathroom.

RIGHT A wide-plank reclaimed wood floor extends from the bedroom to the adjoining bathroom for a unified feel. This rustic finish is easier to maintain in the bathroom, as any water damage would only add to the lived-in feel of the wood.

Laminate tiles can look like ceramic tile, wood, or even stone. Here they imitate slate floor tiles, complete with faux grout lines where the pieces meet.

Laminate

Made popular by the brand Pergo®, laminate flooring can look like wood, ceramic, or stone. It's actually made of fiberboard with a printed image (usually of wood grain) on top and sealed with a plastic resin. Laminate is thin and can sound hollow when walked on, although underlayment installed between the subfloor and laminate reduces the noise. Laminate can be installed as a floating floor over existing materials, but be sure to caulk all the edges so that moisture doesn't seep underneath. Laminates do hold up to water better than wood, but they cannot be refinished.

ARCHITECT KATHRYN ROGERS ON

The Maintenance Factor

When choosing materials for the bathroom, consider whether you are the type of person who will do the care and maintenance needed for products like wood, cork, linoleum, and stone. "Wood floors are great in bathrooms that kids don't use, as children will ruin the floors when they splash around. It's a nice option, but it requires that the homeowner keep it as dry as possible. If you're not willing to be diligent about this, choose another material."

Linoleum and Vinyl

Linoleum and vinyl are often considered inter-changeable, but they are very different products. Linoleum was popular in the early 1900s, but when vinyl flooring came on the market at a lower price point in the 1940s, droves of homeowners ditched the old-fashioned linoleum. Today linoleum is enjoying a resurgence, in part because it is an eco-friendly product. Made of linseed oil, cork dust, wood flour, tree resins, ground limestone, and natural pigments, linoleum flooring itself, plus the manufacturing and disposal of it, involves no environmental toxins.

While linoleum used to come only in drab shades, today you can choose from a wide array of colorful hues. Linoleum is a great choice in period homes, many of which may still have an old linoleum floor in the kitchen or laundry area—proving its longev-ity. Linoleum is made from a mix of materials that are pressed together, so if you scratch it, you won't see a different color underneath. In fact, scratches can be filled in easily with some shavings of a left-

over tile mixed with wood glue. Like stone, linoleum is porous, so you'll want to apply a couple of coats of sealer after installation (even if you bought sealed tiles) to keep water from seeping into the seams, and reseal it about once a year.

Vinyl flooring is inexpensive, widely available, and moisture and stain resistant, and it comes in a broad range of patterns and colors. The patterns are printed on top, so scratches usually mean you'll need to replace the tile. Many building experts are now warning consumers about the environ-mental and health risks associated with vinyl floor-ing because it is made of PVC (polyvinyl chloride). While vinyl flooring may offgas, or release, relatively low amounts of volatile organic compounds (VOCs) into the air once it's installed, a dangerous chemi-cal called dioxin, which is a by-product of PVC, is released into the air during the manufacturing of vinyl flooring and can also be released if the prod-uct ever catches on fire. So when you consider the entire life cycle of the product, it is not an eco-friendly choice.

ABOVE LEFT Specks of blue, cream, and black create a textural pattern in this linoleum bathroom floor.

ABOVE RIGHT This beige linoleum floor mimics the look of stone, but it is softer and warmer underfoot.

OPPOSITE PAGE In a crisp blue and white bathroom, vinyl tiles in a checkerboard pattern make for a low-maintenance floor.

Cork

Cork flooring is a versatile, attractive, eco-friendly product that is not often recommended for bathroom use but can perform well if properly maintained. Made of pre-consumer recycled material (from the cork-stopper manufacturing process), cork is also sustainable, as the bark of the cork oak tree can be harvested every nine years without harm to the tree. Look for manufacturers that make cork tiles in a variety of colors and patterns and that use water-based pigments, varnishes, and adhesives so there are no chemicals offgassed into your home.

In addition to having eco characteristics, cork is soft and warm to walk on with bare feet; resists denting; reduces noise, heat transfer, and vibrations; and is naturally insect repellent. Installing cork is a great DIY project, especially if you buy prefinished and preglued varieties. Cork can be damaged if flooded by water, but the occasional splash or moisture that moves relatively quickly through the room will not harm it (though you will be hard-pressed to find a manufacturer that will warrant its product in the bathroom, as it can't control how the surface will be taken care of). Like other resilient flooring, cork should be sealed after installation and resealed about once per year.

Rubber

While there are a wide variety of rubber tiles and sheet flooring products on the market, the selection gets much smaller when you're looking for something suitable for indoor use. Rubber flooring that contains black recycled tires is better for exterior applications because of the strong smell and volatile organic compounds (VOCs) it will emit. Choose rubber flooring made without PVC (polyvinyl chloride), ideally containing natural rubber or recycled SBR (styrene-butadiene rubber). Most of these come in a variety of colors, which, along with their more forgiving surface, makes them a great alternative to ceramic tiles for kids' bathrooms. Ask the manufacturer if you need to seal the flooring to protect it from moisture.

Carpet

Carpet is not the best choice for most bathrooms because it can get moldy when repeatedly exposed to moisture. It is also difficult to keep clean. If you have a large master bathroom with a dressing area or walk-in closet, carpet can work nicely there. To take the chill off a tile or concrete floor, use area rugs that can be thrown into the washing machine.

ABOVE Rich chocolate cork tiles give this bathroom a sophisticated feel in addition to making the room warmer and quieter.

OPPOSITE PAGE, TOP LEFT Cork can also be made to mimic other materials. In this example, cork planks are designed to look like a eucalyptus wood floor.

OPPOSITE PAGE, TOP RIGHT The wall-mounted sink and rubber tile with a slip-resistant raised pattern make this a universally accessible bathroom (see pages 214–215).

OPPOSITE PAGE, BOTTOM LEFT Jute or sisal rugs can sustain exposure to water and humidity better than synthetic fibers. This rug works beautifully in a Bali-style bath with cool blue walls and a square concrete vanity.

OPPOSITE PAGE, BOTTOM RIGHT This bathroom has a separate dressing area that can be closed off during a steamy shower, making low-pile carpet a comfortable flooring choice for this section.

CLOCKWISE FROM LEFT These 12-by-24-inch cork tiles are set in a geometric pattern.

These multicolored linoleum tiles have a mottled surface.

The palettes of these two terrazzo floors come from the colors of the stones, glass, and resins used.

These porcelain tiles have a slightly textured surface that mimics natural stone.

Flooring at a glance

Ceramic Tile

- **Pros:** Broad range of sizes, shapes, and colors; durable; water resistant
- **Cons:** Must choose styles with enough strength for floors; can be slippery; cold underfoot; grout is high maintenance
- **Price:** $–$$
- **Installation:** DIY friendly; can be installed over existing floor if smooth and stable
- **Green Issues:** Look for tiles made of recycled materials, or for salvaged or surplus tiles that would otherwise go to waste

Porcelain Tile

- **Pros:** Can mimic the look of stone; strong; water resistant
- **Cons:** Cold underfoot; grout is high maintenance
- **Price:** $–$$
- **Installation:** Installs like ceramic tile, but you'll need a diamond-blade wet saw to cut through it
- **Green Issues:** More eco-friendly than natural stone

Glass Tile

- **Pros:** Stylish; unique; beautiful color palette
- **Cons:** Must choose styles with enough strength and slip resistance for floors (either mosaic or a textured finish); grout is high maintenance
- **Price:** $$–$$$
- **Installation:** Use smooth, white thinset if tiles don't have a solid sheet backing; otherwise you'll see mortar through the tiles
- **Green Issues:** Look for tiles made of recycled glass

Stone

- **Pros:** Luxurious; range of colors and patterns
- **Cons:** Color and veining can vary from what you see in the showroom; heavy; cold underfoot; must be resealed regularly
- **Price:** $$–$$$
- **Installation:** Make sure subfloor is strong enough to handle the weight
- **Green Issues:** Most varieties are shipped in from overseas, contributing to carbon emissions; choose one that's quarried close to home

Concrete

- **Pros:** Can be stamped, textured, and colored; easy to clean
- **Cons:** Cold and hard underfoot (but can be warmed up with a radiant-heat system); must be resealed regularly

- **Price:** $$–$$$
- **Installation:** Hire an experienced contractor to pour a solid concrete floor; concrete tiles install like ceramic but should be sealed before installation
- **Green Issues:** Consider substituting some of the portland cement with fly ash; use recycled aggregates

Terrazzo

- **Pros:** Durable; waterproof; tiles with resin binder don't need to be resealed
- **Cons:** Heavy; cold and hard underfoot
- **Price:** $$–$$$
- **Installation:** Tiles install like any others; if poured in place, require an experienced professional
- **Green Issues:** Choose varieties that contain pre- and post-consumer recycled glass or other recycled materials rather than stone

Bamboo

- **Pros:** Looks similar to hardwood but is less expensive; can be sanded and refinished several times
- **Cons:** Limited color choices; must be resealed regularly to avoid water damage
- **Price:** $–$$
- **Installation:** Installs just like hardwood
- **Green Issues:** Imported from Asia (carbon emissions issues); some varieties contain formaldehyde adhesives that offgas

Wood

- **Pros:** Wide variety of colors, grains, and plank widths; soft and warm underfoot; can be sanded and refinished several times
- **Cons:** Must be resealed regularly to avoid water damage; can crack and buckle if bathroom is allowed to become too steamy on a regular basis
- **Price:** $$–$$$
- **Installation:** Available as a nail-down, glue-down, or floating floor; installation best left to a professional
- **Green Issues:** Use water-based, low-VOC (volatile organic compound) stains and finishes; buy Forest Stewardship Council (FSC)–certified or reclaimed wood flooring

Laminate

- **Pros:** Looks similar to hardwood, ceramic, or stone but can be less expensive
- **Cons:** Can't be refinished
- **Price:** $–$$
- **Installation:** Challenging DIY installation; floats over existing subfloor
- **Green Issues:** Look for manufacturers that have FSC-certified or recycled-content fiberboard cores; avoid those that contain formaldehyde adhesives that offgas

Linoleum

- **Pros:** Wide variety of colors; made of natural materials; durable; biodegradable; warm and soft underfoot
- **Cons:** Linseed oil in linoleum gives off a slight odor that some people find objectionable (decreases over time); must be resealed regularly
- **Price:** $–$$
- **Installation:** DIY friendly
- **Green Issues:** A wholly green material, from cradle to grave, although it is currently manufactured only in Europe (transportation emissions issues)

Vinyl

- **Pros:** Warm and soft underfoot; doesn't need to be resealed
- **Cons:** Damaged tiles will need to be replaced
- **Price:** $
- **Installation:** DIY friendly
- **Green Issues:** Made of PVC (polyvinyl chloride), which has serious environmental and health issues (see page 47)

Cork

- **Pros:** Warm and soft underfoot; resists denting; has insulating qualities
- **Cons:** Must be resealed regularly
- **Price:** $–$$
- **Installation:** DIY friendly
- **Green Issues:** Uses a renewable and preconsumer waste material; choose manufacturers that don't use formaldehyde adhesives and do use no-VOC finishes

Marble, a popular and colorful stone, is available in variously sized tiles, mosaics, and decorative border pieces.

Rubber

- **Pros:** Durable; water and slip resistant
- **Cons:** Certain types made with recycled tires have an odor; some styles are more suited to commercial and outdoor installations
- **Price:** $–$$
- **Installation:** DIY friendly
- **Green Issues:** Choose ones that are made with recycled and renewable materials that do not offgas

Carpet

- **Pros:** Wide variety of colors and textures; soft and warm underfoot
- **Cons:** Hard to keep clean; not recommended for moist areas
- **Price:** $–$$
- **Installation:** Wall-to-wall requires professional installation
- **Green Issues:** Choose carpets made of natural materials like wool, or that contain recycled material

Walls and Ceilings

Walls painted in a rich cocoa help to highlight the unusual shape and pitch of the roof in this sunny bathroom.

Use bathroom walls to make the space seem clean and restful by painting them a solid neutral color, or add texture to the room by tiling, wallpapering, or faux-painting them. Often overlooked, ceilings can contribute to the style of the room with the right color paint or even tile.

Paint

The fastest and least expensive way to add color to your bathroom is with paint. If you have a lot of different colors represented already, you may want to paint the walls a neutral color so that some of the other elements in the room can shine. Or use paint to add a splash of color on one or two walls if your bathroom is predominantly white.

Large paint displays containing thousands of color chips can be intimidating. Some paint lines now offer oversized paint chips or small samples of popular colors to help make your decision easier. Most paint chips are still printed color, however, so they will be very close to the color of the paint but won't have the same sheen (how matte or glossy the finish is) or texture of your wall. Painting a small area of the wall in the sheen you want and viewing it at various times of the day using natural and artificial light is the only way to really know what the color will look like. If you can't find a small sample in the color you want, you can always buy a quart and look for other uses for the leftovers if it turns out not to be the right color.

Semigloss and satin sheens are easier to clean than flat. But the higher the gloss, the more you'll see any imperfections in the wall surface.

Eco-friendly, nontoxic paints are much easier to find than they used to be. Opt for a no-VOC latex paint tinted with no-VOC pigments when possible to preserve your indoor air quality.

ABOVE Some people shy away from saturated colors in small spaces, but in a bathroom with natural light and crisp white trim, this glaucous blue paint is a showstopper.

LEFT A plastered wall in terra-cotta warms up a Balinese-style bath.

Ceramic, Porcelain, and Glass Tiles

There are even more choices in ceramic tile for walls than for floors, as you can use handmade and specialty glazed varieties that aren't strong enough for floor use. Glazed tiles are easy to keep clean, and often a design or color will come in a variety of shapes, sizes, and trim pieces. When you're tiling around a freestanding tub, for example, you'll need bullnose tiles with a finished edge for the side, and corner pieces for inside and outside corners. For a backsplash, you may want a line of trim tiles between the main expanse of field tiles, plus a tile with a finished edge for the top. Architect Dennis Fox warns his clients not to fall in love with a specific tile without making sure the manufacturer also has the trim pieces the design calls for. Always check the whole line before making a decision.

Beyond solid colors and glazed finishes, decorative ceramic tiles can provide color and texture on a wall. They can be handmade, embossed, or even painted with a design that creates an image when all the tiles are put together. Make a statement by installing decorative tiles as a backsplash or across an entire wall, or use them sparingly to add interest in a field of solid-colored tiles. Often their price is prohibitive enough that you'll want to limit their use to accents.

You might not always be able to tell the difference between solid-color ceramic and porcelain wall tiles. Porcelain can also look just like natural stone, giving you a high-end feel for a more down-to-earth price.

Made of sand and water, glass tiles are a natural choice for the bathroom. They're easy to maintain, and they reflect light beautifully. Glass tiles can be clear, frosted, or opaque. Some have a backing that provides the color, while others are tinted during the manufacturing process, which is truly an art form. Like ceramic and porcelain, glass tiles come in a variety of sizes, including mosaics, and some have matching trim pieces.

Any of these tiles can be put on the ceiling as well, either just in the shower area where they will help protect the surface from water damage, or across the room.

OPPOSITE PAGE, LEFT Handmade glazed ceramic tiles cost more than machine made, but when they are used across an entire wall, the variation in color on each individual tile creates a watery, tactile effect.

OPPOSITE PAGE, RIGHT Crackle-finish ceramic tiles with a border of ceramic and tumbled stone surround this alcove tub.

ABOVE LEFT Porcelain tiles can mimic many other materials. In this case a bamboo pattern is printed on the face.

ABOVE RIGHT Narrow, horizontal glass tiles in three shades of blue-gray create an eye-catching, reflective surface.

TOP An unusual stone can give your bathroom a unique look—at a hefty price. This lavender-colored stone, called "azul macaubas," covers the walls of this shower surround.

MIDDLE Tawny-colored tumbled slate provides a warm hue for the walls and slip resistance for the floors in this shower, which looks onto an enclosed deck.

BOTTOM These "timera" travertine tiles have a slightly pillowed edge that makes you want to reach out and touch them. The cocoa brown color sets off a white and chrome vanity beautifully.

OPPOSITE PAGE Interior designer Heidi Pribell loves to mix and match tiles. Here, she used gray and white marble tiles as mosaics across the walls, set them in a diamond pattern as a chair rail, and repeated them on the floor with onyx accents. Less expensive white ceramic subway tiles fill up the rest of the wall, while ceramic trim and molding pieces at the bottoms, middle, and tops of the walls pull the whole design together.

Stone

As with stone floors, stone installed on walls and ceilings will need to be kept sealed to protect it from stains and moisture, but the extra maintenance can be well worth the effort. A bathroom with floor-to-ceiling stone tile has a classic and elegant look, but it comes at a high price. If you need to keep the cost down, consider using stone only as a backsplash, or as a strip of accent tiles in a field of porcelain or ceramic.

While using large, smooth stone tiles on the floor would be too slippery, they're perfect for walls and you will have less grout to maintain. You can also install slabs of stone cut to fit the width of your walls and finished with a decorative edge. You won't have any grout lines, but these solid pieces are heavy and expensive.

Architect Kathryn Rogers suggests taking all the wall tiles you buy out of the boxes and laying them on the floor to decide how you want the tiles positioned. With some types of stone, the veining pattern can vary dramatically, so you'll want to decide on the layout before installing the tiles on the wall.

Tumbled stone has a rough, pitted surface and an Old World look. Slate is naturally water resistant with a textured surface, making it a great choice for custom showers if you want the same material on the floor and the walls. Travertine has a more uniform color than most other natural stones and is often used when marble or granite would be too busy. Granite is waterproof and provides a more consistent pattern than marble.

If you're using two different kinds of stone on the wall, make sure they are the same thickness. Otherwise, you may have to build up the wall in some places to make them even.

This horizontal wainscot was custom milled from Medex®, a wood-composite panel product with no added formaldehyde that resists moisture. The white oak hardwood floor and cherry vanity are protected with a marine-grade urethane finish.

Wainscot

Wainscot (or wainscoting) is a wall covering that starts at the floor and extends one-third or two-thirds up the wall; tile wainscoting often has a decorative cap piece at the top. It is a good choice for kids' bathrooms because ceramic, porcelain, or glass tile will be easier to clean than painted drywall. Stone wainscoting is popular in master and spa baths as a way to incorporate stone on the walls without having the expense of taking it all the way to the ceiling.

Wood wainscoting is often seen in Arts and Crafts, Cottage-style, and Victorian homes. It will need to be painted or sealed to prevent it from being damaged by water and humidity— be sure to prime or seal the back as well. Classic beadboard wainscot pieces have tongue-and-groove edges that fit together and are nailed in place. Some manufacturers sell plywood panels that look like beadboard but come in 4-foot sections, which makes the installation go a lot faster. They are also less expensive than individual pieces of

hardwood, but they are an option only if you plan to paint rather than stain. You can also find wainscot pieces made of medium-density fiberboard (MDF), which will stand up to moisture better than hardwood or plywood. However, standard MDF contains formaldehyde, which will offgas in your home for several months. Look for MDF that contains no formaldehyde and cover it with a no-VOC paint for a healthy, eco-friendly option. One such product, called Medex®, is also resistant to moisture, making it a great choice for the bathroom.

Wallpaper

Most often seen in half baths, especially those trying to evoke a period look, wallpaper is another way to add color and texture to the bathroom. Wallpaper made of vinyl with a paper backing is the best choice for moist areas, but it can be problematic in other ways. If moisture is able to seep behind the wallpaper at a loose seam or from a small cut, mold can start to grow underneath and you may not realize it before you have a large amount and a serious health hazard on your hands. There are also environmental and health issues relating to vinyl itself (see page 47). If you do install vinyl wallpaper, be vigilant about openings or keep it away from wet areas. You can buy vinyl-free wallpapers, some of which even use nontoxic inks, but they will not fare well if exposed to moisture, so use them only in half baths.

TOP LEFT Tongue-and-groove bead-board panels in crisp white surround the sink and toilet areas, stopping short of the glass tiles in the shower surround.

BOTTOM LEFT In a half bath where large mirrors are not a necessity, an intricate wallpaper pattern like this map of the world can entertain guests.

RIGHT The combination of wainscot and wallpaper in this yellow and white bathroom has a cheerful, feminine look. While large patterns can overwhelm small rooms, choosing a design that uses just two colors and keeping it to the top half of the wall allows the pattern to be lively rather than intrusive.

CLOCKWISE FROM BOTTOM LEFT
These glass mosaic tiles have an iridescent finish.

These ceramic subway tiles with a crackle finish have matching border and trim pieces.

Fireclay's Debris series tiles are made from recycled glass and gravel, and asphalt waste material.

Yellow beadboard wainscot creates a homey feel in a country-style bath.

Use wallpapers like these, which are silk-screened with water-based inks, in half baths that won't get steamy.

Wall Finishes at a glance

Paint

- **Pros:** Quick and inexpensive
- **Cons:** Won't cover up damage on a wall
- **Price:** $
- **Installation:** Great DIY project
- **Green Issues:** Buy low- or no-VOC (volatile organic compound) paint to avoid problems with indoor air quality

Ceramic Tile

- **Pros:** Broad range of sizes, shapes, and colors; durable; water resistant
- **Cons:** Grout is high maintenance
- **Price:** $–$$
- **Installation:** Install over new or existing greenboard, cement backerboard, or drywall; mid-level DIY project
- **Green Issues:** Look for tiles made of recycled materials, or for salvaged or surplus tiles that would otherwise go to waste

Porcelain Tile

- **Pros:** Can mimic the look of other materials; strong; water resistant
- **Cons:** Grout is high maintenance
- **Price:** $–$$
- **Installation:** Install over new or existing greenboard, cement backerboard, or drywall; mid-level DIY project
- **Green Issues:** Often more eco-friendly than the material it is mimicking, such as stone

Glass Tile

- **Pros:** Stylish; can use larger glass tiles on the wall than on the floor
- **Cons:** Grout is high maintenance
- **Price:** $$–$$$
- **Installation:** Use smooth, white mastic if tiles don't have a solid sheet backing
- **Green Issues:** Look for tiles made of recycled glass

Stone

- **Pros:** Luxurious; range of colors and patterns
- **Cons:** Color and veining can vary from what you see in the showroom; heavy; must be resealed regularly
- **Price:** $$–$$$
- **Installation:** Best left to a professional
- **Green Issues:** Most varieties are shipped in from overseas, contributing to carbon emissions; choose one that's quarried close to home

Use expensive hand-painted or stone tiles as accent pieces to add interest to your design while keeping overall costs down.

Wainscot

- **Pros:** Can be done with wood or tile
- **Cons:** If wood, must be kept sealed to avoid moisture damage
- **Price:** $–$$
- **Installation:** Midlevel DIY project; wood goes up quickly if you're using panels
- **Green Issues:** Buy MDF (medium-density fiberboard) panels that do not contain formaldehyde, or use reclaimed or Forest Stewardship Council (FSC)–certified wood; finish with a low- or no-VOC paint or stain

Wallpaper

- **Pros:** Quick way to add color and texture to walls; works well in period homes
- **Cons:** If moisture gets behind wallpaper, you can have a mold problem without knowing it
- **Price:** $–$$$
- **Installation:** Good DIY project
- **Green Issues:** Vinyl wallpaper is made of PVC (polyvinyl chloride), which has serious environmental and health issues (see page 47); use nonvinyl wallpaper in powder rooms and half baths

The beauty of paint is that you can opt for bold colors knowing you have nothing to lose. If you don't like it, paint over it.

Simple Serenity

Painted white walls, large windows, and a frameless mirror all contribute to the open, airy feeling of this bathroom. A practically invisible glass shower door protects the room from splashes, but the side facing the tub is open so the edge of the tub can serve as a ledge or seat for the person in the shower. An operable window assists the bathroom fan in removing steam from the room.

The combination of natural materials and light in this modern bathroom would give anyone a more positive view of the world at the start of the day. Architect Beth Gensemer created this master bath as part of an addition to an old Spanish-style home, whose charm she set out to preserve but not mimic. "My clients felt that the walnut and travertine gave the bathroom a feeling of warmth while letting them have a more modern, light-filled room," Beth said.

Naturally occurring pits and holes in the travertine countertop, floor, and wall tiles were filled with a resin before installation and then sealed so that the material would hold up better in a bathroom. The handmade "watery" glass mosaic tiles were installed flush with the drywall so that a cap piece to hide the edge of the top row wasn't necessary, allowing the straight lines and hard edges of the design to continue uninterrupted.

The room is small, so the homeowners decided to forgo a double vanity in order to make room for a separate shower and tub. The toilet is in a separate niche. To visually enlarge the space, Beth brought the frameless wall mirror all the way down to the countertop, which also makes the room seem brighter.

The Elements

- **Flooring and Tub Surround:** 24-by-24-inch travertine with bone-colored grout

- **Walls:** Handmade glass mosaic tiles with white grout; white paint

- **Vanity:** Custom floating frameless in walnut

- **Countertop:** Travertine slab

- **Sink:** Enameled cast-iron square undermount

- **Sink Faucet:** Widespread with a polished-chrome finish

- **Bathtub:** Undermount acrylic

- **Bathtub Faucet:** Widespread with a polished-chrome finish

- **Finishing Touches:** Flat, round cabinet pulls in polished chrome

Pattern Play

Classic fixtures in polished nickel and a Carrera marble countertop are in keeping with the cool tones of the room. The polished mahogany toilet seat matches the door to the bathroom.

OPPOSITE PAGE, LEFT
A handheld showerhead perches delicately on its cradle atop this vintage-style tub faucet.

OPPOSITE PAGE, RIGHT
"I chose this deep and narrow bathtub because it looks like a classic Roman tub that would have originally been carved out of marble even though it's really cast acrylic," designer Heidi Pribell explains.

Interior designer Heidi Pribell is an expert at mixing and matching various colors, shapes, and patterns of tile. Although she often combines ceramic, stone, and glass tiles in the same design, she used all ceramic tiles in this Boston bathroom. Heidi loves to play with pattern, as evidenced by the square grid on the floor combined with the diamond pattern on the wall leading to cream subway tiles set in a running bond pattern. Hand-painted blue decorative tiles in trim, border, and cap pieces undulate across the walls and around the mirror.

The Elements

■ **Flooring:** Square ceramic tiles in white and two shades of blue with a light gray grout

■ **Walls:** Blue, white, and cream ceramic tiles in assorted shapes and designs with bone-colored grout

■ **Vanity:** Custom painted face-frame with translucent ribbed glass panels

■ **Countertop:** Carrera marble slab

■ **Sink:** Enameled cast iron undermount

■ **Sink Faucet:** Widespread with porcelain handles

■ **Bathtub:** Cast-acrylic soaking tub

■ **Bathtub Faucet:** Wall-mounted with handheld showerhead

■ **Toilet:** 1.6 gpf gravity-assisted

■ **Finishing Touches:** Wall-mounted soap holder, towel bars, and egg-shaped cabinet pulls in polished nickel; bath caddy; mahogany toilet seat with handles; beveled mirror; sheer drapes

Chapter 3
Cabinets and Countertops

We expect a lot of our bathrooms. They should be beautiful, easy-to-clean respites from the rest of the world—plus be able to store clean towels, dozens of toiletries, accessories, medicine, and stuff you may use only a couple of times a year. To avoid clutter, it's crucial to get organized and then find vanities or freestanding furniture that will help you stay that way. The cherry on top is the countertop, which can add elegance, down-to-earth utilitarianism, or cutting-edge style.

Countertop fabricators can create custom edge details to make your counter look thicker than the slab really is. This white composite countertop sits on a custom gray vanity with extra-wide drawers.

Cabinets

Simple, hard-edged pulls match the sleek and modern style of this frameless vanity, as does the concrete countertop. The flat slab doors don't have any recessed or raised areas where moisture can get trapped.

J ust because you may have had a large vanity in your old bathroom doesn't necessarily mean you'll need to replace it with something the same size. Take this opportunity to go through all the cabinets and drawers and throw away or donate anything you don't use. Check expiration dates and throw out any nontoxic materials you may have (toxic products like nail polish remover and some medications will have to be taken to a hazardous-waste facility). Once you've purged, you're in a much better position to assess your storage needs and decide on the right number of shelves and drawers. Or you may decide you don't need a vanity at all and opt for a pedestal or wall sink (see pages 104–106) or a piece of freestanding furniture (see page 73).

Styles

You may be asked early in the remodeling process whether you are interested in frameless or face-frame cabinets. This information helps designers, cabinetmakers, and retail-store salespeople figure out the general style you're going for. Frameless, or European-style, cabinets are most common. You can identify frameless cabinets by noting whether the drawer and door faces cover most or all of the surface area of the actual cabinet box and if the door hinges are hidden when the doors are closed. Considered more contemporary, frameless cabinets

Cabinet Finishes

S tained wood cabinets withstand dings and generally hold up to moisture in the bathroom better than painted cabinets—but beware of wood veneers, as they can peel back over time. "Just make sure you have a good lip on the counter so that water isn't streaming down the cabinet doors," Kathryn says. Water can't pool up on the cabinet doors and drawer faces if you use flat slabs instead of recessed or raised panels.

come in a variety of door styles, ranging from simple slabs with a flat surface area to recessed and raised panels. Most stock cabinets feature frameless construction.

Face-frame, or American-style, cabinets have doors and drawer faces that generally sit flush with the cabinet box or are partially offset with a lip over the cabinet box. The overall effect is more traditional because this is how cabinets were constructed in older homes. It's a look that works well in period, vintage, or Cottage-style bathrooms, but face-frame cabinets are more expensive to build because they take more skill and time, and you will lose a little drawer space because of the area that the frame takes up.

These face-frame cabinets take up the entire wall, so towel racks were attached under each sink.

Stock

Found at home improvement centers and some kitchen and bath stores, stock cabinets are a relatively inexpensive option. The companies that manufacture them produce a fixed number of styles, colors, and wood choices so they can mass-produce the cabinets and sell them for less money. Cabinets sold as bathroom vanities are typically 32 inches tall and between 18 and 21 inches deep, although you can also choose to buy kitchen cabinets, which are usually 34 inches tall and 24 inches deep, for use in the bathroom. Stock cabinet sizes increase in increments of 3 inches.

You can shop for new stock cabinets and install them the same day, whereas semicustom and custom cabinets can have long lead times. Stock cabinets made of particleboard and covered with plastic composites such as laminate or melamine will be the cheapest, but particleboard is more prone to warping and moisture damage than veneered plywood or medium-density fiberboard (MDF), so it's a good idea to pay a little more for better materials.

Look for stock cabinets that feature dovetail construction (rather than having pieces that are glued or stapled together) and drawers mounted on ball-bearing tracks so they pull all the way out smoothly.

If premade stock cabinets exceed your budget, consider ready-to-assemble (also called RTA) stock cabinets, which come disassembled in a box with all the hardware you need to construct them. Do factor in the amount of time it will take you to put them together, or money you'll spend to hire someone to assemble them.

Semicustom

When available stock cabinets don't have the style, finish, or accessories you want, consider working with a semi-custom cabinet manufacturer. Typically, you'll communicate with this supplier through a retail salesperson at a home improvement center, or through a designer or an architect. Semicustom cabinet companies will allow you to select from a list of wood types, stain and paint colors, door and drawer styles, decorative finishes such as crackle glazes and distressed wood, hardware, and built-in storage solutions. You can get a more custom look this way, and possibly even upgrade to all-wood construction. But the sizes will still run in 3-inch increments, and you'll still be limited to each company's menu of options. Unless you are looking for something to fit an odd space or you have a rare wood species in mind, however, semicustom should be able to provide what you need. These companies are outfitted with state-of-the-art equipment, so you will generally receive your order within 6 weeks.

TOP LEFT Assemble the cabinets yourself to save a little money.

MIDDLE LEFT Open the drawers to see if they feature dovetail construction, as the interlocking pieces in this example show.

BOTTOM LEFT Some stock and semicustom cabinet manufacturers offer pullout storage solutions such as this seemingly decorative side panel that extends to reveal narrow shelves perfect for bottles or a curling iron. An electrician can install a receptacle inside any cabinet to keep clutter off the countertop.

OPPOSITE PAGE, TOP Stock cabinets come in a range of wood finishes and can be jazzed up with interesting pulls. These floating cabinets provide a unique look at a reasonable cost.

OPPOSITE PAGE, BOTTOM Semicustom cabinet companies offer more extras, such as decorative paint finishes, furniture-style feet, and trim options. Mix and match pieces for the storage combination that suits your space.

Custom

When you or your designer works directly with a local cabinet shop, you are not only supporting a local business but you will also get exactly what you want with no compromises. While stock and semicustom cabinets are available in set sizes, a custom cabinet can cover as much or as little area as you'd like with not an inch wasted to filler strips (those pieces of finished material you get with stock and semicustom cabinets to make it look as if the cabinet extends to the wall when standard sizes aren't big enough to fill an area).

Custom cabinets also allow you to get a bit more creative with finishes, moldings, hardware, wood species, and styles. Architect Beth Gensemer often works with custom cabinetmakers to build floating vanities in the size and style she wants (see pages 62–63). Floating vanities have a clean look, and you can see the flooring material from wall to wall. "You lose a little storage space, but it really opens up a small room," Beth says.

Custom cabinets also allow you to choose more eco-friendly materials, such as Forest Stewardship Council (FSC)–certified wood and nontoxic finishes (although a few semicustom manufacturers are also starting to offer these materials). You can even have a custom shop create cabinets from reclaimed wood, as shown on pages 92–93.

It's worth getting a quote on the cabinets you want from a local shop before deciding on semicustom cabinets, because quite often the prices are

INTERIOR DESIGNER TERRELL GOEKE ON

Eco-Friendly Cabinets

Terrell Goeke is a certified manufacturer of eco-friendly cabinets, and shops like his are held to high environmental standards. "Everything is green, from the doors and drawer faces to the formaldehyde-free cabinet boxes," he explains. Terrell must follow strict recycling measures for waste generated during the manufacturing process. He even ships the cabinets wrapped in blankets so there is no cardboard to get rid of. Ordering eco-friendly cabinets is a great way to support those suppliers who are working to generate less waste and protect old-growth trees, plus your family won't be breathing in any toxic chemicals from standard cabinet finishes and adhesives.

This vintage dresser and hutch was transformed into a bathroom vanity that fits perfectly in a tight niche. Metallic tiles form a backsplash, and the top was replaced with a matte solid-surface counter.

comparable. Small shops generally don't have the same machinery that large manufacturers do, nor do they have the same number of carpenters on staff, so depending on the time of year and the popularity of the custom cabinet shop you choose, your order can take anywhere from 4 to 12 weeks.

Furniture

There's no rule that bathroom vanities must have been built for that purpose. If you have an extra freestanding cabinet or desk, a carpenter or cabinetmaker may be able to retrofit it as a bathroom vanity. Wood tops can be replaced with stone slabs, top drawers removed to allow for a sink, and backs cut out to allow for plumbing hookups. Dressers, bookshelves, and dressing tables can also be used as additional storage in the bathroom—particularly when you opt for a pedestal sink and want to create more of a period look than conventional cabinetry would provide. As with standard vanities, stained and sealed hardwood will fare better in the bath than painted wood. Give existing wood furniture a coating of marine-grade polyurethane sealant to protect it from damage and it will last a long time.

Storage

Most wall niches can be only about 4 inches deep, but because there is a closet on the other side of this wall, the designer was able to construct generous 10-inch shelves on one end of the tub alcove for towels and bath toys.

While all bathrooms must be equipped to store everyday items such as shampoo bottles, toothbrushes, and toiletries, most are also called upon to house guest towels, extra toilet paper, and cleaning supplies. Plus it's nice to have some display areas for a vase of flowers or scented candles. Combine several storage solutions, including cabinet inserts, shelves, and wall hooks, to accommodate what needs to be kept in your bathroom.

Cabinet Inserts

There have been great innovations in storage in the past decade, particularly in systems built to make kitchen cabinets and drawers more useful. Interior designer Terrell Goeke encourages clients to utilize these kitchen storage systems, such as stainless-steel baskets on drawer glides or pullout units for trash or laundry, in the bathroom. "These systems are great for bathrooms because they're metal instead of wood. Set a hot dryer in a wooden drawer and it can burn the wood. With a metal insert in a larger drawer or cabinet, however, there won't be that problem," Terrell explains. There are storage systems for nearly every imaginable scenario, including a pull-out, U-shaped metal basket that wraps around plumbing and makes the most of under-sink space.

Shelves

In a piece of freestanding furniture or mounted directly to the walls, shelves provide open storage for everything from toiletries to towels. Wall-hung shelves can solve practical issues such as where to put toothbrushes when you have a sink with no surrounding countertop.

Niches

Wall niches provide a minimalist approach to storage. Instead of having shelves that protrude out into the room, wall niches recede. Most homes have between 14 and 22 inches of empty space between wall studs. Cut away the drywall in areas where there aren't pipes or wires running behind the wall, and you can gain a 4-inch-deep area in which to install narrow shelves or set a few bottles. Because they aren't very deep, wall niches are typically used to hold shampoo and conditioner bottles in showers, to display items like candles or vases, or to store delicate bottles and boxes.

In small spaces, you can also use wall niches to add a few more inches to shelves. Builder Mark De Mattei likes to create a wall niche over a toilet and have shelves come out 5 inches past the wall. When you make use of the space in the wall, the shelves don't extend too far out over the toilet and you have a more usable 9-inch-deep shelf for magazines.

ABOVE A narrow freestanding cabinet with open shelves provides extra storage in a bathroom with a pedestal sink.

RIGHT Shaped to wrap around pipes, this pullout wire shelf holds cleaning supplies in a bathroom vanity.

BELOW LEFT Decorative metal brackets add some flair to a simple glass shelf.

BELOW RIGHT Niches are particularly popular in showers. Place them where they won't be regularly sprayed by water.

Baskets and Bins

Especially in larger bathrooms, having a few attractive baskets on the floor can help free up cabinet space and give you a place to store extra toiletries or towels. A large basket can act as a hamper to keep discarded clothes from piling up, though lidded hampers are best in bathrooms to keep clothes dry. Smaller baskets are great for cotton balls and swabs that can get lost in large drawers. Keep two or three small baskets on the countertop for items that would otherwise clutter the space.

Stackable bins are an inexpensive storage option that will keep contents on display. Their scooped-out fronts provide easy access—a great solution for keeping bath toys organized. Use them in shared bathrooms to hold toiletries for multiple kids.

Hooks and Pegs

When you have the extra wall space, adding a few hooks or pegs in the bathroom will give you a place to hang your bathrobe or the outfit you're about to change into. Be sure to install hooks and pegs into a wall stud so they can hold a good deal of weight, and at a height that people won't hit them with their heads as they walk by. In a kids' bath, hang the hooks low on the wall but slightly above head height. You can keep moving them up the wall as the children grow.

Hooks can also be used for towels, although they don't allow wet towels to dry as quickly as towel racks do.

TOP Use a small wire basket like this one to arrange a movable set of toiletries when guests will be using a shared bathroom.

BOTTOM This metal rail system with movable hooks is typically used for hanging kitchen utensils over cooktops. Here it holds bathroom towels and toiletries.

OPPOSITE PAGE, TOP LEFT Instead of cabinet doors and drawers, this vanity has open cubbies equipped with woven baskets.

OPPOSITE PAGE, TOP RIGHT Use lightweight, waterproof baskets to corral kids' bath toys. Placed on an open shelf or on top of a bench, they will be reachable for little ones.

OPPOSITE PAGE, BOTTOM LEFT This antique coat rack was given a new life in a bathroom.

OPPOSITE PAGE, BOTTOM RIGHT Hung low on a wainscot wall, these hooks are within easy reach of the tub and shower.

Countertops

This teal green tile countertop uses curved cap pieces for edging; small square pieces surround the undermount sink. One row of more expensive Spanish-style tiles runs around the room. The black quarter-round cap piece creates a clear visual divide between the tiles and the painted wall above.

Afteryour floor and wall choices, the countertop has the next biggest design impact in a bathroom. The larger the counter, the larger the impact, although small counters give you the opportunity to use more expensive materials and can be a focal point despite their diminutive size. Remember that countertops work in tandem with sinks and faucets—the right-sized holes may need to be drilled depending on the material you choose—so these decisions should be made at the same time.

Ceramic Tile

Countertops will take some abuse, so you need to select ceramic tiles that are rated for this purpose. Floor tiles will certainly be strong enough, as will porcelain tiles. Some art tiles are too delicate for use on the countertop, and those with raised patterns can be hard to clean. Both are eye-catching options for the backsplash, however.

Ceramic tiles don't need to be resealed and are impervious to water, heat, and stains, but the grout that holds the tiles together will require some maintenance. Apply grout sealer regularly; otherwise you may get some discoloration from mold or spills.

As with wall tiles (see pages 54–55), you'll want to pick a ceramic tile that has a complete line of accessories such as bullnose edges and trim pieces. You can also edge the countertop with wood or metal trim when there are no ceramic edging pieces in the design you choose.

Glass

Glass tiles are available in squares and rectangles, and also as mosaics, in which small pieces in one shade or a rainbow of colors are mounted on a mesh sheet, creating a seamless look. Both options work for countertops, although mosaics have a lot more grout to maintain. You don't have to worry about the slip factor with countertop tiles, so you can choose ones with a smooth finish, but you do need to select glass tiles that are strong enough for countertop use.

There are also solid glass countertops available in several finishes. Some manufacturers use recycled glass, but either way, the countertop itself is recyclable. You can leave the glass clear and see the floor and plumbing below, put a piece of steel or copper between the glass and vanity, or even install LED lights on the backsplash wall to illuminate the glass. These thick slabs are strong, easy to keep clean, and won't be damaged by personal-care products, because glass is naturally nonporous. While they can be scratched, the slight texture of the glass will make the scratches less visible.

TOP Ice blue glass mosaic tiles cover the countertop and extend into a tiled wall that also includes white and ocean blue.

BOTTOM In an all-white bathroom, this frosted glass counter with integral sinks has a hygienic, almost industrial look that works well with all the glass and chrome.

Stone

A natural stone slab countertop is one of the more expensive options, though you can get a similar look by installing stone tiles with extremely narrow grout joints in a color that matches the tiles. Another way to get a stone countertop without going over budget is to ask local stone yards and fabricators for scrap. "There are almost always pieces big enough for bathroom vanities left over from material used for kitchen countertops. Stone yards are often willing to sell the scrap for lower prices, and you're utilizing something that may otherwise be discarded," says interior designer Lou Ann Bauer.

Whether slab or tile, natural stone is porous and will need to be resealed regularly. While stone counters aren't as difficult to protect in the bathroom as they are in the kitchen, you will need to be careful not to spill any personal-care products that contain oil or alcohol. As with stone floors, it's best to be realistic about yourself before committing to a stone countertop. If you're not exactly a neat freak, you might be happier in the end with another type of counter. Of course, stone has been used as a countertop material for centuries by people who didn't expect things to look flawless over the years. So if a little scratch or stain here and there won't bother you, then you have nothing to worry about.

Fabricators can give stone slabs a variety of surface treatments; options include stone that has been polished, tumbled, or honed. Interior designer Heidi Pribell likes to use acid-washed marble or limestone countertops in the bathrooms she designs. "In this process, the softer parts of the stone are worn away, creating a sense of patina. The surface undulates with an irregularity that feels warm and aged," she says.

Visit a stone yard to view dozens of varieties, each with its own coloration and veining. When you work with a local fabricator and stone yard to create a custom countertop, you usually get to pick your own slab. Like slices of bread in a loaf, each slab will have a slightly different appearance, so the one you choose will be uniquely yours.

Fiber Cement

A few manufacturers are producing fiber-cement slabs in an effort to create a countertop that has the rustic elegance of solid concrete or stone but doesn't weigh or cost as much. They are made of cement mixed with various fillers such as recycled glass and paper and need to be resealed regularly.

OPPOSITE PAGE, LEFT Soapstone has a greenish gray color and is more durable than most natural stones. Here, the fabricator also used soapstone to create an apron-front sink.

OPPOSITE PAGE, RIGHT A "floating" counter with no cabinetry highlights the beauty of the stone. Regular ³/₄-inch slabs can be made to look thicker with a mitered edge on the front and sides.

ABOVE LEFT Black and white tumbled marble in a checkerboard pattern provides a visual frame for a glazed black vessel sink.

ABOVE RIGHT Squak Mountain Stone is a fiber-cement countertop made of cement, recycled paper, and recycled glass. It has a rustic, varied appearance and is hand-cast into slabs that can be fabricated in any dimension.

Solid Surface

Traditionally made of plastic with a mineral filler, solid-surface countertops can be shaped and molded into any design. They are available in neutral or hot colors, as well as in patterns that resemble stone. Solid-surface countertops are durable, easy to maintain, and almost impossible to damage. Because the color and pattern extend all the way through the slab, scratches can be sanded out. You can now get solid-surface counters made with a small amount of recycled content.

There are also solid-surface countertops made of pressed paper that is sealed with resin and then baked. Some manufacturers use paper or wood pulp from sustainable forests and others use up to 100 percent postconsumer-waste recycled paper and petroleum-free resin, so there are a range of green options. While pressed paper may not sound durable, it's harder than wood, heat resistant to 350 degrees, and stain resistant. As with plastic solid-surface countertops, scratches can be sanded away. Pressed-paper countertops are available in a variety of colors, slab sizes, and thicknesses, and they have a matte, slightly mottled finish that resembles soapstone.

Interior designer Terrell Goeke often uses solid-surface countertops when the cabinets are made of an exotic wood that has a lot of pattern to it so that he doesn't have competing patterns. "Choosing solid surface is a great and practical way to use color, and you can also get bright colors in a matte finish, which is hard to find," he says.

Laminate

Made of a thin layer of plastic bonded to particleboard or plywood, laminate counters are more affordable than many other countertop choices and are available in hundreds of patterns and colors. Look for brands that offer recycled or FSC-certified content. Unlike solid-surface countertops, laminate has visible seams. Flush and undermounted sinks should not be installed in a laminate countertop, because it's too difficult to ensure that water won't seep into the wood substrate. The best choice for a laminate surface is a self-rimming sink (see page 99) that overlaps the counter with a well-sealed caulk edge.

OPPOSITE PAGE This easy-to-clean solid-surface countertop is an excellent choice for a bathroom that gets a lot of use.

TOP RIGHT The white solid-surface counter in this kids' bath doesn't compete with the strong pattern on the floor.

BOTTOM RIGHT A beveled edge detail dresses up this laminate countertop. Unlike with solid-surface or stone, you can where the pieces come together in laminate.

Stone and Glass Composites

For people who are concerned about the maintenance requirements of natural stone, there is another option that will give you a very similar look, at a similar price, but without the hassle. Stone composite, also referred to simply as quartz, is made of ground-up natural quartz mixed with polymers and epoxy. While natural stone slabs vary in color and veining, you can buy one quartz slab today and another a year from now and, depending on the mix of materials you choose, you probably won't be able to tell the difference between them. The surface won't be damaged by heat and is hard to scratch, and you won't have to worry about spills. Little pieces of stone or glass suspended in each slab create an interesting visual texture, and the binding agents can be tinted anything from cream to bright red, giving you looks ranging from subdued to shocking.

CaesarStone offers a wide range of neutrals and a few hot colors in varying textures—from tiny specks to large chunks of quartz—and there's a line that contains recycled content. Architect Beth Gensemer is a big fan of CaesarStone countertops. "I love the natural, light colors, plus a composite material like this requires a lot less maintenance than marble," she explains. In addition to its standard quartz countertops, Silestone produces slabs that have the unique patterning of natural stone, a line with metallic aggregates, and a design called Volcano that has a lightly indented pattern across the surface, proving that the possibilities with quartz are almost limitless.

There are also a few small eco-friendly manufacturers such as IceStone that use 100 percent post-consumer recycled glass in a cement binder to create truly one-of-a-kind surfaces that are made in America. Unlike with quartz, there are no plastic binders in these countertops, so they will need to be resealed periodically.

TOP Composite countertops can be clean and simple, like this white quartz aggregate in a white base, or bold with geometric and colorful patterns.

BOTTOM Amber Pearl IceStone is made of portland cement and recycled glass, plus tiny pieces of post-industrial recycled abalone shell to give it that extra sparkle.

OPPOSITE PAGE You can't get natural stone in solid hot pink, but it's an option with composite countertops.

LEFT This custom-made concrete countertop with side panel features dual integral sinks.

OPPOSITE PAGE, TOP LEFT Because metal is so often used in industrial settings, it has the right aesthetic for sleek and modern bathrooms like this one, which also doubles as an exercise room.

OPPOSITE PAGE, TOP RIGHT This polished wood countertop and backsplash are made of the same material as the custom cabinetry and mirror frame, creating a cohesive and elegant look.

OPPOSITE PAGE, BOTTOM A warm wood counter plays off coffee-colored tiles and a wood-framed window. The curved design wraps around the room, serving as a base for the sink and storage ledge.

ARCHITECT
KATHRYN ROGERS ON

Concrete Countertops

Bathrooms with more of a rustic design do best with concrete countertops. "Some of my clients have been disappointed by concrete after a few years when it's become stained and cracked. If people are okay with having the material show signs of wear and tear and the design can support it, then concrete countertops can work nicely."

Concrete

Sculptural and artistic, with the heavy permanence of a solid stone slab, concrete countertops can be tinted in earth-toned shades or bright colors and they generally have a mottled, matte finish, though gloss finishes are also possible. Concrete countertops can feature anything from handprints of your kids to botanical patterns, or have an aggregate finish in which stone or glass is mixed in.

Unlike most other surfaces, concrete countertops may develop hairline cracks over time. Some people accept them as part of the look, but if cracks and visible wear and tear will bother you, then choose something else. Certain toiletries can stain concrete counters when spills are left to sit for hours, but resealing the counter regularly will help prevent stains.

Concrete countertops can be poured in place or purchased as pre-made slabs. Counters that are poured in place are often pure concrete and therefore very heavy. Some manufacturers offer lighter-weight concrete mixes that are more economical to ship and can be carried upstairs (by several strong people) for the installation. Sonoma Cast Stone offers a line called EarthCrete that is lighter in weight than traditional concrete, environmentally sustainable, and contains an additive that makes it stain-free without resealing.

Consider ordering an integral sink with your concrete countertop, meaning the counter and sink are formed as one piece with no seams. Concrete artists can create these sinks in unique shapes and depths to be features of your overall bathroom design (see pages 120–123).

Metal

Stainless-steel counters are often seen in restaurant kitchens because they are easy to clean and sanitize and difficult to damage—all equally good qualities for a bathroom. As with concrete, you can order a stainless-steel countertop with an integral sink. Stainless steel is more affordable than concrete or composite countertops. It will get scratches, but those simply add to the aesthetic. Much more expensive and high maintenance are specialty metals such as copper and zinc, but their unique looks can be worth the money and frequent polishing if they work best with the style of bath you're creating.

Wood

Warm and natural, wood counters are sometimes the best choice in rustic, cabin-style, or traditional bathrooms. To protect wood from splashes and spills, reseal it regularly. By working with a custom shop, you can get a wood countertop in practically any species and size. And if it ever gets stained or damaged, you can always have it refinished, just like a wood floor.

TOP LEFT A standard-sized integrated backsplash covers the area between the countertop and the mirror.

TOP RIGHT A mirror that extends from the countertop to the ceiling can act as a backsplash, as mirrors are easy to keep clean and they protect the wall surface from moisture.

BOTTOM RIGHT Raised tiles add contrast without necessarily introducing a new color.

Backsplashes

To complete the look of your countertop, and protect the wall above it from splashes, you will need a backsplash. This is a great place to use a high-priced, big-impact material, as long as it won't be difficult to keep clean. Any of the countertop materials described in the previous pages will work as a backsplash. For a harmonious design, you can simply use the same material from the counter for the backsplash, or you can choose something completely different.

The standard height for a backsplash is 4 inches, but it can be as minimal as you'd like or extend all the way to the ceiling. If you plan to incorporate a wall-mounted faucet, be sure you plan out the backsplash material carefully so you don't end up with a grout line or seam right where the faucet needs to be.

INTERIOR DESIGNER
TERRELL GOEKE ON

Metal

Metal is great from an aesthetic standpoint—it's a rigid material that adds sparkle. "The backsplash is a perfect place to incorporate metal into the design, as it's easy to clean and less likely to get scratched there than it would be as a countertop."

Standard backsplashes are 4 inches tall. This marble example has a traditional ogee edge to complement a delicately detailed faucet.

KALLISTA

CLOCKWISE FROM LEFT Corian solid-surface countertops come in a wide range of styles and patterns.

Granite is one of the harder natural stones and will require less maintenance than marble as a countertop.

Laminate can have a mottled appearance similar to stone, as well as patterns not found in nature.

Countertops at a glance

Ceramic Tile

- **Pros:** Broad range of sizes, shapes, and colors; water, heat, and stain resistant
- **Cons:** Limited to styles that are strong enough for countertop use; grout can be hard to keep clean and must be resealed regularly
- **Price:** $–$$
- **Installation:** DIY friendly
- **Green Issues:** Look for tiles made of recycled materials, or for salvaged or surplus tiles that would otherwise go to waste

Glass

- **Pros:** Stylish; unique; beautiful color palette
- **Cons:** Limited to styles that are strong enough for countertop use; grout can be hard to keep clean and must be resealed regularly (not an issue for solid-glass countertops)

- **Price:** $$–$$$
- **Installation:** If the tiles don't have a solid sheet backing, use white mastic; otherwise you'll see it through the tiles
- **Green Issues:** Look for tiles made of recycled glass

Stone

- **Pros:** Luxurious; range of colors and patterns
- **Cons:** Some types are easy to scratch; color and veining can vary from what you see in the showroom; heavy; some types need to be resealed regularly
- **Price:** $$–$$$
- **Installation:** Stone slabs require professional installation; stone tiles are a midlevel DIY project
- **Green Issues:** Choose a variety quarried close to home to reduce carbon emissions; select a leftover or salvaged slab that would otherwise go to waste

Fiber Cement

- **Pros:** Less expensive way to get the look of stone or concrete
- **Cons:** Must be resealed regularly to avoid stains; limited colors available
- **Price:** $
- **Installation:** Requires professional installation
- **Green Issues:** Select manufacturers that incorporate recycled materials into the concrete mix

Solid Surface

- **Pros:** Available in hundreds of colors and patterns; can be made in any shape; can include integral sink(s); highly durable; scratches can be sanded out
- **Cons:** Plastic types are made from petrochemical-based materials
- **Price:** $$

- **Installation:** Requires professional installation

- **Green Issues:** Look for manufacturers that use postconsumer recycled paper and toxin-free resin rather than plastics

Laminate

- **Pros:** Available in hundreds of colors and patterns; can order as one piece with integral edge and backsplash

- **Cons:** Made from petrochemical-based materials; relatively easy to scratch; stains and scratches cannot be repaired; has visible seams

- **Price:** $

- **Installation:** Can be purchased ready-made or constructed onsite by experienced DIY'ers

- **Green Issues:** Look for manufacturers that offer Forest Stewardship Council (FSC) certification or recycled content

Stone and Glass Composites

- **Pros:** Nearly infinite range of colors and patterns depending on material used; heat, scratch, and stain resistant

- **Price:** $$–$$$

- **Installation:** Requires professional installation

- **Green Issues:** Look for manufacturers that use recycled content

Concrete

- **Pros:** Wide variety of aggregates, surface finishes, shapes, and colors; integral sinks available

- **Cons:** Can develop hairline cracks; heavy; most types must be resealed regularly to avoid stains

- **Price:** $$–$$$

- **Installation:** Hire an experienced contractor for best results

- **Green Issues:** Ask your contractor to substitute some of the portland cement with recycled fly ash to reduce CO_2 emissions by keeping the ash out of landfills

Metal

- **Pros:** Unique; stainless steel is hygienic and stain resistant

- **Cons:** Copper and zinc must be polished frequently; all show watermarks if water is allowed to sit on surface

- **Price:** $–$$$

- **Installation:** Requires professional installation

- **Green Issues:** Look for manufacturers that will create countertops out of salvaged metal

Wood

- **Pros:** Wide variety of species and stains; can be sanded and refinished

- **Cons:** Not heat or water resistant; must be resealed regularly

- **Price:** $–$$

- **Installation:** Professional installation is recommended

- **Green Issues:** Buy FSC-certified or reclaimed wood; use water-based, low-VOC (volatile organic compound) stains and finishes

Fiber cement has a rugged, natural appearance that's more earthy than stone and wears better than pure concrete.

Eco-Bath

The freestanding cabinet reflected in the mirror and the floating vanity were both constructed from reclaimed Douglas fir. Random-patterned ceramic tiles in five shades of green surround the vanity and lead into the corner shower.

OPPOSITE PAGE, LEFT The dual-flush toilet sits between the exterior wall and the free-standing cabinet. Green paint picks up on the color of the tiles on the opposite wall.

OPPOSITE PAGE, RIGHT Architect Kathryn Rogers chose an integral porcelain sink and counter unit because it doesn't compete with the patterns on the walls and cabinets. The custom medicine cabinet features glass shelves and a frameless rectangular mirror.

When architect Kathryn Rogers's clients approached her about remodeling their bathroom, they told her they wanted it to be as eco-friendly as possible. That mindset led them to use reclaimed wood for the bathroom's custom vanity and freestanding cabinet. The builder, Lawrence Construction, selected Douglas fir beams salvaged from an old city hall building. Instead of going to the landfill, these 6-by-6-inch beams were planed, jointed, sanded, and turned into something beautiful. Plus, reclaimed wood is more stable dimensionally and will hold up better than new wood in a moist environment. Kathryn also used paints and stains that are low in VOCs (volatile organic compounds), put lights on occupancy sensors to reduce electricity use, and installed water-saving fixtures. A graywater system allows shower and sink water to be reused for irrigation by transporting it in separate pipes that lead to mulch basins in the garden.

The Elements

- **Vanity:** Custom face-frame floating cabinet in reclaimed Douglas fir

- **Countertop and Sink:** Integral porcelain

- **Sink Faucet:** Widespread in satin nickel

- **Flooring:** Brazilian blue-gray slate tiles with gray grout

- **Walls:** 1-by-3-inch handmade ceramic tiles with gray-green grout; low-VOC paint

- **Shower:** Custom with satin nickel-framed glass doors; rain showerhead and handheld showerhead in satin nickel

- **Toilet:** Two-piece dual-flush

- **Lighting:** Square wall sconces and ceiling fixture framed in satin stainless steel

- **Finishing Touches:** Custom medicine cabinet; satin nickel pulls and shower door handle; glass shelf above toilet

Sublime Storage

Resembling a fine piece of furniture, the vanity takes up very little floor space but has a strong presence in the room.

OPPOSITE PAGE, LEFT
The toilet niche is surrounded by cabinets yet maintains an open feel.

OPPOSITE PAGE, RIGHT
Tiling around the mirror anchors it to the tub area. Recessed niches on either side of the faucet line up perfectly with the rim of the slipper tub.

Architects Jessica Allee and David Gast created this refined and cozy master bath by reconfiguring a separate toilet compartment and bathroom into one space. Despite its diminutive size, there is no shortage of storage in this bathroom. The recessed mantel over the vanity provides a wealth of hidden shelves and drawers for accessories. Below a Carrera marble countertop are eight drawers and a rounded cabinet door that plays off the round sink and mirror above. Another recessed cabinet was installed in the toilet alcove, and a narrow wall-hung cabinet above the toilet takes advantage of the high ceilings to provide even more storage space.

The soft palette of white and gray creates an open feeling, while a 4-by-4-foot operable skylight floods the room with filtered light and provides natural ventilation. The home's Edwardian detailing is referenced in the simple lines of the subway tile wainscot, and the owner's appreciation of the Victorian style is reflected in the period fixtures and tub. With its shoulder-level water-line, the enameled and burnished metal slipper tub is fit for royalty. The bathing experience is complete with an electric floor-heating mat under honed Carrera mosaic tile, as well as a recessed toe-kick heater.

The Elements

- **Cabinets:** Custom-built face-frame, painted and topped with crown molding

- **Countertop:** Honed Carrera marble

- **Flooring:** 1½-inch honed Carrera marble mosaic tile with white grout

- **Walls:** Subway tile wainscot and gray paint

- **Sink and Faucet:** Undermount round vitreous china; widespread in polished nickel

- **Bathtub and Faucet:** Cast-iron slipper tub; widespread wall-mount faucet and handheld showerhead in polished nickel

- **Toilet:** Two-piece with vintage styling

- **Finishing Touches:** Glass knobs and pulls; beveled mirrors; polished-nickel towel racks; sconce light fixtures with shades; magnifying mirror

Chapter 4

Sinks, Faucets, and Toilets

Perhaps you've never given much thought to these necessary and everyday bathroom staples, but today there are more choices than ever. A sink can be small and white and sit beneath the surface of the countertop unnoticed, or it can make a splash on top of the counter, becoming a focal point of the room. Faucets should relate to your shower and bath fixtures in terms of style and finish, while decisions on toilets should be based primarily on water efficiency.

A trough sink with his-and-hers faucets sits atop a mirrored vanity in this light-filled bathroom.

Sinks

Undermount sinks allow this antique table-turned-vanity with marble counter to take center stage in the bathroom.

No longer limited to the simple white sink of the past, consumers now have a diverse selection of sizes, colors, materials, and installation types from which to choose. Architect Beth Gensemer likes using rectangular sinks because they echo the lines of tiles or stone and other linear surfaces in the bathroom, even though they do take away a little counter space.

While sinks can be either subdued background players or featured performers in your bathroom design, their most important role is to be functional. Every bathroom will have a different definition of functional. Will your sink need to be large enough for two people to share, small enough to fit in a tight space, or deep enough not to splash back when you're washing your face? If you have a vanity (see pages 68–73), you'll need to decide on a self-rimming, undermount, or vessel sink. Otherwise, you'll be debating among a pedestal, wall-mount, or console sink.

Self-Rimming

Also called drop-in sinks, self-rimming sinks are inherently traditional but can be found in more modern shapes and materials. A hole is cut into the countertop, and either the sink sits with its rim supported by the counter or the rim is installed so it's flush with the surrounding surface. In either installation, it's important to make sure the seam between the sink and the countertop is well sealed with caulk. If it isn't, water might seep in and damage countertop substrates. An overlapping rim does make the countertop a little harder to clean, because you can't simply wipe water and suds directly into the sink as you can with an undermount or an integral sink.

Undermount

These sinks are mounted under the countertop so that its surface is uninterrupted and easy to wipe down. Undermount sinks have a clean and modern style and work best with slabs that you can cut into and polish the edge of, such as stone, solid surface, concrete, and composites. Countertop materials that sit on a wood substrate, such as ceramic or glass tile, will require that you carefully tile around the edge of the sink to protect the substrate. Undermount sinks don't work with plastic laminate counters.

TOP LEFT The gently rounded edges on these self-rimming sinks reinforce the soft, feminine style of this cream-colored bathroom.

BOTTOM LEFT The fabricator of this stone counter created a step-down frame for the polished silver undermount sink.

TOP RIGHT A pair of square self-rimming sinks sits under two tall, framed mirrors. The glass shelf below provides extra storage.

BOTTOM RIGHT Turquoise mosaic tiles frame the edge of a square undermount sink. The mirror extending down to the counter visually doubles the amount of blue in the room.

Above Counter

Quite popular in recent years, above-counter (commonly referred to as vessel) sinks sit on top of or are set partway into the countertop surface, looking much like a giant mixing bowl on a kitchen counter. You will of course still need to drill a good-sized hole in your countertop to allow water to drain into pipes below. These sculptural sinks can be true works of art made of blown glass or hammered metal, or sturdy-looking basins made of vitreous china. Depending on how deep or narrow they are, above-counter sinks can be a bit messy if they don't catch every splash of water. Sometimes this is not a problem, but if the countertop material you purchase shouldn't have standing water on it very often, an above-counter sink may be a better choice for a bathroom that doesn't get heavy use.

Interior designer Terrell Goeke warns that because an above-counter sink is usually paired with a wall-mounted faucet, you'll need to make your final sink and faucet decisions before the rough plumbing stage. "Wall faucets have to be a certain height and distance from the wall to work with a vessel sink, so you can't leave this decision until the very end the way you may be able to with other types of sinks," he says.

TOP A sculptural piece of rough carved stone is perched atop a smooth metal counter for an interesting juxtaposition of textures.

BOTTOM The deep sides of these square above-counter sinks contain most splashes.

OPPOSITE PAGE, TOP LEFT Mounting the faucet to the side of this bowl-shaped above-counter sink allows for a narrow shelf on the wall above.

OPPOSITE PAGE, TOP RIGHT Fire clay sinks are available in many colors and styles. This black above-counter sink features circular ridges that make it look like a piece of pottery.

OPPOSITE PAGE, BOTTOM LEFT Glass mosaic wall tiles in peaches and blues provide a shimmery backdrop to this "Tennessee pink" marble sink.

OPPOSITE PAGE, BOTTOM RIGHT An interesting mix of earthy materials are tied together by a steel above-counter sink. Brushed metal was also used on the mirror frame—only the wall-mount faucet provides some shine.

Held up by two metal bars, this wall-mounted solid glass countertop and integral sink keep the room feeling bright and open.

Integral

With concrete, solid-surface, metal, wood, and glass countertops, you have the option of ordering an integral sink. There are also some one-piece porcelain sink countertops that technically fall into this category. Integral sinks are easy to keep clean because there are no joints into which water and dirt can seep. Stone fabricators can also make sinks using the same type of stone as the countertop and glue the pieces together with tight seams to mimic an integral sink.

TOP LEFT This integral porcelain sink is set on a floating white cabinet and has ample counter space on either end.

BOTTOM LEFT This smaller-than-average rosy pink concrete integral sink works well in a half bath.

TOP RIGHT Concrete fabricators can get creative with integral sinks, as they aren't limited by standard molds and sizes. In this example, water spills into a reservoir that leads to a pipe under the sink.

BOTTOM RIGHT This carved-wood countertop with integral sink even has an integral cup holder. A glass panel ensures that the water doesn't flow out.

ARCHITECT KATHRYN ROGERS ON

Integral Sinks

Integral sinks offer a lot of design flexibility in that they don't necessarily need a cabinet or table legs below. "I often use Duravit integral sinks, which are made of porcelain. They don't stain, and they're so easy to clean."

Pedestal

Traditionally seen in vintage and cottage-style bathrooms, pedestal sinks can work in any style of bath and are available in a variety of profiles, widths, and heights. They consist of two pieces: the column and the bowl. The column can partially hide the plumbing that comes out of the wall and extends up to the sink and faucet. The bowl can have a small lip on which to set toothbrushes, a wide lip that can accommodate toiletries, or no lip at all. While pedestal sinks are great for small bathrooms where a full vanity would take up too much space, you'll most likely need to add a combination of smaller storage solutions such as wall-hung shelves or a narrow piece of freestanding furniture.

TOP Four decorative tiles create a simple backsplash behind an antique pedestal sink.

BOTTOM This unique pedestal sink has a scalloped edge. The wooden table to the side serves as counter space for towels and toiletries.

OPPOSITE PAGE A basket placed between matching square pedestal sinks holds extra towels. To make up for the lack of counter space, glass shelves were installed just below the medicine cabinets.

Wall Mount

Wall-mount sinks used to be seen only in commercial applications, but homeowners have come to appreciate their slight stature and ability to make tiny bathrooms appear larger. Manufacturers are now making them in a variety of styles and sizes, including ones that fit into tight corners. Like pedestals, some have a tiny amount of space around the sink for a bar of soap, while others give you more elbowroom. Most have a small wraparound area below the sink that covers pipes, but you can get one that doesn't. You'll need to decide on this style of sink before the walls are closed up, as they require extra bracing between the studs to give the sink's bolts something solid to grab onto.

Console

Console sinks have the look of a piece of furniture and come in as many styles, sizes, and finishes as tables do. Traditionally, the countertop is attached to the wall and two legs in the front help hold the weight, but you can also get a four-legged console that looks even more like a table. Consoles can have one or more sinks and as much or as little counter space as you desire. You can buy a console that comes with a countertop and sink or build your own with table legs and choose the counter and sink you like best.

LEFT A minimalist wall-mount sink sits at the end of a long and narrow shower, allowing for shaving and tooth brushing while bathing.

OPPOSITE PAGE, TOP Porcelain console sinks are available in many configurations. The bar on this example provides extra stability and also serves as a towel rack.

OPPOSITE PAGE, BOTTOM Two elongated sinks are mounted on a floor-to-ceiling glass wall. The crosscut wood flooring material in the center of the room is also used for open-air shelves leading into the bathroom.

Console Sinks

Console sinks give the bathroom a more open look than closed vanities do. "I like consoles with an open shelf on the bottom. It's a great place to put rolled-up or folded towels."

CLOCKWISE FROM LEFT
Vitreous china is often the material used for hand-painted, artistic sinks.

Stone sinks are unique but expensive.

Concrete sinks are usually part of the cast countertop.

Sink Materials at a glance

Enameled Cast Iron

- **Description:** Formed in molds, sprayed with enamel powder, then fired
- **Pros:** Easy to clean; resists chipping and cracking; comes in a wide variety of colors
- **Cons:** Heavy
- **Price:** $–$$
- **Installation:** Self-rimming; undermount; above counter; wall mount; integral

Porcelain Enamel

- **Description:** Made of a mixture of minerals heated and sprayed onto a metal surface, then fired
- **Pros:** Easy to clean; resistant to stains
- **Cons:** Abrasive cleaners can scratch surface
- **Price:** $–$$
- **Installation:** Self-rimming; undermount; above counter; wall mount; integral

Enameled Steel

- **Description:** Made of enamel-coated sheet metal
- **Pros:** Lightweight; looks similar to cast iron
- **Cons:** Light weight makes it noisy; susceptible to chipping
- **Price:** $–$$
- **Installation:** Self-rimming; undermount

Vitreous China and Fire Clay

- **Description:** Made of kiln-fired clay
- **Pros:** Scratch and stain resistant
- **Cons:** Susceptible to chipping; heavy
- **Price:** $$
- **Installation:** Self-rimming; above counter; wall mount

Cast Polymer/ Engineered Stone

- **Description:** Made of ground stone and polyester resin
- **Pros:** Looks like marble or granite
- **Cons:** Inexpensive gel-coated varieties can blister and crack around the drain hole
- **Price:** $–$$
- **Installation:** Self-rimming; undermount; above counter; integral

Solid Surface

- **Description:** Made of plastic with a mineral filler, usually as part of the countertop
- **Pros:** Easy to clean; scratches can be sanded out
- **Price:** $$
- **Installation:** Integral; undermount

Toilets

Kohler's Archer one-piece elongated toilet has a gravity-assisted flush and is Water-Sense certified.

You might have an existing toilet that works well and looks fine in your new bathroom, but if it uses more than the federally mandated 1.6 gallons per flush, you should replace it anyway. So-called "low-flow" toilets came out in the 1990s and didn't make a good first impression. Manufacturers have since addressed early problems, and you can now get an efficient toilet that doesn't use 3.5 gallons (or even as much as 7 gallons for really old toilets) each time you flush.

According to the Environmental Protection Agency, toilets account for approximately 30 percent of residential indoor water use. A WaterSense (see page 112) high-efficiency toilet that uses less than 1.3 gallons per flush will save approximately 4,000 gallons and $90 per year on the water bill for a family of four—even more if the toilet being replaced leaks or was manufactured earlier than 1980. To determine how old your current toilet

is, lift the lid and look inside the tank for a stamped date. Your new toilet will quickly pay for itself in lower water bills, plus some local utilities also offer rebates for replacing old water-guzzling appliances and fixtures.

Gravity Assisted

Standard toilets simply release water from the tank into the bowl, using the force of gravity to carry waste down the trapway and into the sewer pipe. All new gravity-assisted toilets use no more than 1.6 gallons of water per flush, but the best low-flow toilets have 3-inch flush valves and wide trapways so that water and waste don't have to move through such small openings. They also have glazed trapways so things move along more smoothly.

ABOVE LEFT The tanks of old-fashioned toilets used to be mounted higher on the wall so water could come down with greater force. While this quaint example looks appropriate with the vintage claw-foot tub, these old models waste water and should be replaced.

ABOVE RIGHT Toto's 1.6-gallon-per-flush toilets feature a wide, fully glazed trapway to practically eliminate clogs. This two-piece model looks great in traditional bathrooms.

Architect Dennis Fox set out to create a bright and open spa bathroom in this house that overlooks a bay. The homeowners did not want any doors in their master suite, so Dennis used objects and thick walls that accommodate built-in storage to separate and define spaces.

A low wall with cantilevered shelves visually separates the toilet alcove and includes a recessed magazine rack. On the other side of the wall, an integral concrete double sink designed by homeowner Mark Lederer and fabricated by Concreteworks slopes to the center to drain. A removable teak shelf hides the drain and provides a surface for toiletries or decorative accessories. Single-lever faucets are mounted to the same green glass tiles used in the shower, tying those two areas together. Below the counter is a single shelf in the same wood finish used throughout the bathroom.

Dennis balanced the light from the large window over the tub and the small glass blocks nearby with the long skylight above the shower, which opens so that steam can escape. Slatted teak duckboards were installed over a recessed shower pan to allow for a level transition to the limestone floor tiles, and floor-to-ceiling green glass wall tiles create a shimmery, watery effect.

Completing the spa-bath experience is a jetted tub situated in front of a two-sided fireplace that also opens onto the master bedroom. The tub can be filled from a deck-mounted waterfall-style faucet or, more dramatically, from a spigot mounted on the ceiling. In this well-designed space, the homeowners can lounge in the tub in front of a flickering fire while gazing out at their water view. They can even crack the window open for a whiff of salty sea air.

The Elements

- **Countertop and Sink:** Integral concrete with sloped bottom and removable teak shelf

- **Sink Faucets:** Wall-mounted in polished chrome

- **Toilet:** Two-piece, 1.6 gpf

- **Flooring:** 12-by-12-inch limestone tiles with white grout

- **Walls:** 12-by-12-inch limestone tiles with white grout; green glass tiles with matching grout; cream paint

- **Fireplace Surround:** Integral green plaster finish

- **Bathtub:** Deck-mounted jetted tub with dual headrests

- **Shower:** Open with glass-tiled walls and slatted teak floor; two rain-style showerheads and two handheld showerheads in polished chrome

- **Lighting:** Dimmable recessed cans

- **Finishing Touches:** Gas fireplace; cantilevered display shelving; recessed magazine rack; wood-framed mirror; glass-block windows; polished chrome wall pegs; recessed niches in the tub platform

The open shower is bathed in light. It features separate fixed and handheld wand-style showerheads that operate independently.

OPPOSITE PAGE, LEFT Gas-fired logs ignite at the flip of a switch to keep the space warm during long soaks.

OPPOSITE PAGE, RIGHT Sleek wall-mounted faucets pour into both sides of a center-sloped double sink.

Chapter 5
Bathtubs and Showers

Most of us look forward to an invigorating shower or a relaxing soak in the tub as the perfect way to begin or end the day. If your bathroom remodel is extensive enough that you are building a new shower or buying a new tub, then you can create spaces that work best for your needs and possibly add spa amenities such as a steam shower. If you're keeping the existing shower and tub, there are certainly ways to give them a makeover as well by replacing the tile, refinishing the tub surface, and upgrading faucets and showerheads.

A pair of double-hung windows with frosted glass allow sunlight to pour into this bathroom through a clear shower door.

Bathtubs

Placed under windows in a second-story bathroom, this undermount tub with smooth stone surround and wood-paneled sides offers excellent views of the treetops. The center-mounted faucet allows two bathers to sit comfortably.

There is an ideal bathtub for everyone, whether you want to sit and soak for hours or quickly get the kids cleaned before bed.

Clients frequently tell builder Mark De Mattei that they don't need a bathtub because they don't use one, but he often sways them with his belief that a tub in a master suite is important for resale value. "Besides, there should be at least one tub in a house, preferably on a first floor, in case someone needs to use it after an injury," he explains.

Before you get started selecting the type of bathtub you want, consider a few logistics. A large and heavy bathtub will impact your remodel more than a standard-sized model. While you shouldn't have to worry about floor strength with a standard tub up to 6 feet long, you might need to add a few extra joists under the subfloor if you're installing a soaking or jetted tub. Consult with your builder or architect on this issue.

A large tub will also quickly empty out most standard-sized water heaters. "In these cases, most people chose to install a tankless water heater so they can never run out of hot water, rather than just upgrading their tank water heater," says architect Kathryn Rogers. So factor in the cost of a new water heater when budgeting for a soaking tub.

Finally, consider the access route. If you're remodeling a second- or third-story bathroom reachable only by a narrow staircase, you won't be able to bring a large tub to the room, unless you're also redoing the roof.

Keeping Your Existing Bathtub

If your existing bathtub has chips or stains or the color is outdated, you may think that the only choice is to get rid of it. But before you pull out the sledgehammer, have a professional tub-refinishing company give you a quote on sprucing up the old tub, which will often cost less than buying and installing a new one.

Chips and cracks in cast-iron or steel tubs with porcelain or enamel finishes can be repaired, and the entire surface can be refinished in whatever color you choose. This requires the use of toxic chemicals, which is why you want to hire a professional and make sure everyone who isn't wearing protective gear stays out of the house during the process and for hours afterward. The technique can vary, but generally the old tub surface is etched or a bonding agent is applied and then several coats of acrylic polyurethane are sprayed on. The finish cures in about four hours and will have the look and feel of porcelain, but it won't last as long as the original finish. Another option is to cover the existing tub with acrylic. A professional will measure your tub and then create and install a seamless acrylic liner that fits perfectly over it.

ABOVE The cast-iron tub in this 1950s-era home was refinished during the bathroom remodel and looks as good as new surrounded by a wide band of blue glass tiles.

RIGHT Standard alcove tubs can be given a more custom look with the addition of a sliding glass shower door.

BELOW This undermount tub's wood-paneled sides have metal mesh inserts. The handheld faucet head makes bathing in the tub easier.

Shopping for a Tub

Never order a tub from a catalog or the Internet. "I strongly recommend that my clients shop for a tub in person because different-sized tubs work for different-sized people. A 5-foot, 2-inch person in a deep tub might feel as if he or she is in danger of drowning, whereas a 6-foot, 2-inch person will have to bend his or her knees in a short and shallow tub. You also can't know whether the back is comfortable unless you sit in the tub."

Recessed, Drop-In, and Undermount Tubs

Recessed, or integral, models are installed against walls on three sides and have a finished front apron. Corner units also have one finished end. The standard size is 5 feet long and 2½ feet wide, though you can find these tubs in slightly larger sizes. Drop-in, or deck-mounted, tubs are much like drop-in sinks—they have a lip that rests on a custom-built tub deck and no prefinished sides. An undermount tub also has no prefinished sides and is installed in a custom tub deck, but the tub sits slightly below the finished edge of the stone or tile surround. All of these tubs are most often found in acrylic, enameled cast iron, and enameled steel (see pages 136–137).

While these options may seem more economical when compared with the price of stand-alone jetted or soaking tubs, architect Beth Gensemer points out that you need to consider the cost of finishing out a basic tub with stone tiles on the side or a slab on top. "Often by the time you factor in the surrounding materials, the price is similar," she says.

Soaking Tubs

A soaking tub can be twice as deep as a standard tub, allowing the water to rise up to your neck. This tub isn't intended for bathing but rather to soak in once you've already showered. Single-person versions don't take up as much space as a standard tub and are often chosen over a jetted tub for small master or spa bathrooms. Make sure you sit in the model you're interested in before ordering, and take into account that filling a soaking tub may require installing a new water heater as well as possibly reinforcing the floor to handle the approximately 800 pounds of combined water and tub weight.

ABOVE A drop-in acrylic tub is a great choice when you want something simple and inexpensive.

OPPOSITE PAGE, TOP LEFT The stone tub deck surrounding this undermount tub extends into the adjoining shower as a ledge to sit on or to hold shampoo bottles.

OPPOSITE PAGE, TOP RIGHT Soaking tubs can be found in a variety of styles. This rustic cabin features a tub shaped like an old wine barrel.

OPPOSITE PAGE, BOTTOM LEFT Set into a hole in the floor, this soaking tub doesn't block the view of the enclosed courtyard through the floor-to-ceiling window.

OPPOSITE PAGE, BOTTOM RIGHT Soaking tubs usually have floor-mounted faucets, but you can also place the tub under a wall-mounted faucet, as was done with this acrylic egg-shaped model.

OPPOSITE PAGE, TOP Whirlpool tubs need an access panel for motor maintenance. This one is barely visible on the side of the tub surround. A wall-mounted tub faucet uses the same water supply pipes as the shower on the other side of the tiled wall.

OPPOSITE PAGE, BOTTOM A two-person jetted tub has headrests on both ends.

TOP This drop-in whirlpool bath is about the same size as a standard recessed tub. The access panel was tiled to blend in with the slate surround, and the motor is housed in the tub deck that extends into the shower.

MIDDLE This deck-mounted tub has 47 air-massage jets around the bottom edge of the tub. You can order one with more jets along the floor for a stronger massage.

BOTTOM Whirlpool tubs can also be used as a shower base when you don't have room for both. This one fits into a deep alcove surrounded by blue mosaic tiles.

Jetted Tubs

Made popular by Jacuzzi®, whirlpool tubs use water jets to massage aching muscles. They come in a wide range of sizes and shapes and can be dropped into a raised deck, set flush with the floor, or placed freestanding. Water jets provide a vigorous massage—you can pick the number and location of jets to get the results you're after. These tubs do require space for a motor, which can be built into the tub deck or placed in an adjoining closet, attic, or basement (thus reducing the noise in the bathroom). Whirlpools require a dedicated electrical circuit, as well as a second circuit if you choose the electrical heating option to keep the water warm longer. Also remember that you can only use bath salts in whirlpool tubs, as bubble bath damages the internal workings.

Air-jet tubs have tiny holes across the bottom and sides that allow pressurized air to shoot into the water. They can be set to give a very gentle champagne-bubble effect or a harder massage that's similar to a water-jetted whirlpool. Because the water is not recirculated in the pipes, you can use bubble bath or bath oils in air-jet tubs. They use a blower to push air through the water, which is quieter than a whirlpool motor.

Both types require some maintenance. Whirlpool tubs need to be flushed out regularly with a special cleaner sold by manufacturers to avoid bacterial buildup in the pipes. Some air-jet tubs dry out the pipes automatically after each use, reducing the likelihood that a problem will arise.

Jetted tubs are available with an amazing number of features and add-ons, including single or double contoured backrests, an infinity edge (allowing water to flow over the sides into a recirculating reservoir), and even chromatherapy, which uses lights to color the water and alter your mood.

INTERIOR DESIGNER
TERRELL GOEKE ON

Jetted Tubs

About half of my clients who install a jetted tub do so for resale value, in which case they put it off to the side. When people really want to use it for themselves, they make it a focal point in the room. I advise clients not to choose models that are larger than 37 by 72 inches, as they get prohibitively expensive and take up space that could be used for other amenities."

ABOVE LEFT This apple green claw-foot tub provides a cheerful burst of color in a black and white bathroom. A handheld showerhead makes it easier to bathe kids and pets.

ABOVE RIGHT A billowy shower curtain lends dramatic flair to a classic claw-foot set in an alcove.

Claw-Foot Tubs

Whether you purchase a new model or refurbish an old one, a claw-foot tub will add instant vintage style to the bathroom. Old models often have holes at one end where the faucet used to be, but new models are generally made without holes drilled into the tub itself and require a floor- or wall-mounted faucet instead. Make sure you know exactly where the model you choose will sit before having a plumber extend the pipes to the right spot.

Many claw-foot tub owners paint their old models interesting colors, and new claw-foots are available in a range of finishes. The decorative feet can be painted, or they can have metallic finishes such as polished brass and chrome to match your faucets and other bathroom accessories. One manufacturer even makes a claw-foot tub with air jets, blending old aesthetics with new technology.

This unique glass surround transforms the claw-foot tub into a shower much more comfortably than a plastic shower curtain would. Water is pumped up through one of three polished chrome rods supporting a large rain-style showerhead.

Custom Tubs

If you have a small or awkward layout, consider hiring a contractor to build a custom tub in the shape and size that works best for the room. A frame built out of 2 by 4s is surrounded by cement backerboard and can be finished in any tile you'd like. Just as with a custom shower, the base will have to be floated (see page 142), which will add to the expense, but constructing it from scratch probably won't cost much more than a good enameled cast-iron tub with tile surround.

Custom tubs can also be made of concrete, wood, or metal with any combination of features and in any size you require. These tubs are works of art and can cost thousands of dollars.

Walk-In Tubs

Standard tubs, whether raised or recessed, can be difficult for people with disabilities or limited strength to get into and out of. A raised walk-in tub provides safety and independence for those who need assistance to take a bath. The door has a watertight seal that won't leak when closed properly. Once the person is in the bath with the door shut, the water can be turned on, and once the tub has drained, the door can be opened again. Look for models with a low step into the tub and a low seat. The floor of the tub is slip resistant, and most models have built-in grab bars and towel racks. The tub can be turned into a shower with the addition of a handheld showerhead on the faucet or a regular showerhead higher up on the wall. You can even get a jetted walk-in tub, which is helpful for people with circulatory problems.

ABOVE Diamond Spas custom-built this stainless-steel bathtub with a contoured base that cradles the body, adding water jets for a unique experience.

OPPOSITE PAGE, TOP LEFT Sail away in this boat-like carved-wood tub amid gorgeous views of a private hillside.

OPPOSITE PAGE, TOP RIGHT Concrete tubs can be cast in any shape or size. This model features a wide ledge for toiletries and a shelf for towels. To achieve a specific hue, from neutral to bold, add pigment when the concrete is mixed or apply an acid stain that permanently bonds to the finished surface.

OPPOSITE PAGE, BOTTOM LEFT Faced with narrow horizontal tiles, this custom tub and shower combination features one sloped side for more comfortable bathing.

OPPOSITE PAGE, BOTTOM RIGHT Walk-in tubs don't take up much floor space. This model by Oceania features variable-speed air jets.

Bathtubs at a glance

Fiberglass
- **Pros:** Lightweight; can be molded into different shapes
- **Cons:** Shows scratches; can't use abrasive cleansers
- **Price:** $

Acrylic
- **Pros:** Lightweight; can be molded into different shapes; has color throughout so scratches won't show
- **Price:** $$

Porcelain or Enamel over Steel
- **Pros:** Lighter than cast iron; resists stains
- **Cons:** Not as durable as enameled cast iron; surface will rust if chipped
- **Price:** $$

Porcelain or Enamel over Cast Iron
- **Pros:** Durable; resists stains; retains heat; water hitting the surface is not as loud as with other materials
- **Cons:** Heavy
- **Price:** $$–$$$

Metal
- **Pros:** Copper and bronze retain heat, keeping bath water warm longer; stainless steel is easy to clean
- **Cons:** Must be vigilant to avoid hard-water marks and patina
- **Price:** $$$

Wood
- **Pros:** Can be carved into any shape from a variety of wood species; teak has natural water-resistant qualities; warm

- **Cons:** Must be resealed regularly and wiped down after each use
- **Price:** $$$

Concrete
- **Pros:** Can be molded into any shape and tinted practically any color
- **Cons:** Cold (unless radiant heat is built in); hard; heavy; must be resealed regularly
- **Price:** $$–$$$

Stone
- **Pros:** Unusual look; most often cultured marble created from marble dust and polyester resin; can also be carved from solid stone
- **Cons:** Cold; hard; heavy; must be resealed regularly
- **Price:** $$–$$$

A 60-inch solid marble soaking tub can weigh up to 1,800 pounds without water, and cost as much as an economical car.

Tub Faucets

The handheld showerhead on this brass deck-mounted faucet makes the tub more functional for bathing.

Whatever style and finish you choose, make sure your tub faucet has solid-brass inner workings so it will last as long as possible.

WALL-MOUNT FAUCETS can be installed either on the side of the tub or on the wall above the tub. If you have an antique claw-foot tub, you may need to buy the faucet through a claw-foot tub dealer to find one that matches the dimensions of the predrilled holes.

DECK- OR RIM-MOUNT FAUCETS are installed through holes drilled either in the rim of the tub or in the surrounding decking material. These faucets allow for more space inside the tub than a wall-mount faucet installed on the tub itself.

FREESTANDING FAUCETS are installed on the bathroom floor adjacent to the tub. Hot- and cold-water supply lines can come out of the floor and meet in a mixing trap before piping water to the faucet, or you can choose a model that mixes the water under the floor so there is just a single pipe reaching up to the faucet.

A HANDHELD SHOWERHEAD is a great addition to a tub faucet if you plan to use the tub for anything other than a relaxing soak. Using a handheld showerhead is much easier than maneuvering under the faucet when you are washing your hair, and it's also really handy for washing kids and pets. It will require a diverter valve, which can be mounted either on the deck, on the wall, or on the tub itself, depending on the system you buy.

ABOVE In addition to having separate hot- and cold-water pipes that extend up from the floor, this freestanding faucet connects to an overflow pipe, which drains the water that rises past this point in the tub.

RIGHT A cross-handled deck-mount faucet in brushed chrome sits on one end of a narrow undermount whirlpool tub.

BELOW This wall-mount faucet has an integrated soap holder.

INTERIOR DESIGNER
LOU ANN BAUER ON

Tub Faucet Placement

Think about how you'll use your tub before deciding where to mount the faucet. "If two people will be using the tub at the same time and sitting at opposite ends, make sure the faucet is mounted at the center of the tub rather than at one end where it would be in the way."

Showers

A solid panel of glass covers about half the length of this tub-and-shower combination, adequately protecting the room from splashes without a full door or shower curtain.

A shower can take up a small corner of the bathroom, share space with the tub, be constructed for two, or double as a sauna.

Tub-Shower Combinations

When there isn't enough room for a separate bathtub and shower, the tub often doubles as a shower. You can buy a prefabricated bathtub-and-shower module, but most people choose to tile the tub surround in a material of their choice.

The main challenge with a tub-and-shower combination is the door. The least expensive option is a shower rod and curtain, but glass shower doors are often preferred. Architect Beth Gensemer often uses frameless glass bifold doors that come in 2-foot pieces and can be folded flat against the walls when you need access to the tub. Other options are to use a fixed glass panel that extends only partway across the tub, or to install a glass panel on one side and a glass door that swings open into the room on the other.

Shower Stalls

Prefabricated shower stalls come in one-piece units or as multiple pieces that can be assembled on site. Ranging in width from 32 to 64 inches, they include the shower pan (floor), walls, and sometimes a ceiling. Doors and faucets are usually sold separately.

ARCHITECT
ANNE LAIRD-BLANTON ON

Recessed Shower Niches

Add recessed niches to the walls in a tub-and-shower combination so you'll have a place to put shampoo bottles other than on the edge of the tub. "Whether you're working with mosaics or 12-inch-square tiles, make sure the niche is sized to work with full tiles. Cut tiles will break up the pattern and your eye will be drawn to them, whereas using only full tiles provides a seamless look."

Most shower modules include sculpted soap and shampoo niches, and some have built-in ledges for sitting. They can be installed between three walls or in a corner and are made of fiberglass-reinforced acrylic, plastic laminate, or synthetic marble. One-piece units are usually reserved for new construction, as they are too big to move through existing doorways. Buying a prefabricated shower stall will be less expensive than creating a custom shower, because it comes with a pan and you don't have to cover the walls with tile or stone.

Besides being relatively inexpensive, prefabricated shower stalls can be installed quickly, and you won't have to regularly maintain caulk or grout in the shower.

TOP LEFT Three wall niches placed low to high allow people of varying heights to reach the soap. The shower is enclosed by sliding glass doors on metal tracks.

TOP RIGHT This prefabricated shower unit fits into a corner but doesn't extend to the ceiling, which gives it a more open feeling.

BOTTOM Built-in ledges for toiletries and a bar for washcloths add a custom touch to this prefabricated shower unit.

Custom Showers

A shower can be built anywhere and in any configuration as long as you have access to plumbing lines and can install or build a shower pan. While your builder can hand-float a shower pan, you'll save some money by opting for a prefabricated shower pan. "Prefabricated pans are safe, watertight, and easy to install, and they come in a variety of attractive finishes," says architect Dennis Fox. "Plus, the money you will save in labor from not having to float a custom shower pan will allow you to use a nicer material on the shower walls." Shower pans come in a range of sizes, but hand-floating the pan may be your only option if you are planning an odd-sized or unusual design.

A new option for custom showers is the infinity drain. Inspired by the trench drain, an infinity drain allows you to pitch the surface in one direction (as opposed to four directions for a standard center drain), opening up a wider range of options in shower floor materials. The drain itself can be anywhere along the run, and there are several lengths, finishes, and styles available. Infinity drains also meet ADA requirements for barrier-free entry showers.

Equip your custom shower with anything you like, such as a bench for sitting or to facilitate shaving your legs, a high window to let natural light in while maintaining privacy, or dual showerheads so two people can shower at once without arguing about who is hogging the water.

Shower Doors

Tempered glass shower doors can be clear, frosted, or etched with a design of your choosing. Framed glass enclosures are less expensive than frameless because they use a lighter-weight glass, but they don't visually recede as well because of the metal tracks surrounding them. The tracks themselves are also hard to keep clean. Frameless glass enclosures are mounted to the walls and floor (or tub) with small clamps that are barely noticeable, but without a frame to catch it, water will drip onto the floor when you open the shower door. While they are beautiful and make your bathroom feel larger, clear glass doors will need to be wiped down after every use if you don't want to see water marks. People tend to keep a squeegee in the shower for this purpose.

OPPOSITE PAGE, LEFT This large custom shower has a wall niche that runs almost its full length and a fixed floor-to-ceiling glass panel. A step allows water to run through a teak slatted floor and into a drain installed at the standard floor height.

OPPOSITE PAGE, RIGHT An infinity drain can be placed anywhere within or along the perimeter of the shower, as opposed to a standard drain placed in the center.

ABOVE LEFT Frosted glass shower doors provide a significant amount of privacy, as evidenced here where they obscure the details of the vibrant orange tiled walls.

ABOVE RIGHT A custom clear glass door that follows the slope of the roof allows an unobstructed view of this showstopping shower covered with shimmering silver mosaic tiles.

Instead of closing off the sloped roof area of this bathroom with a shower door, the designer created an open, curbless shower that extends seamlessly into the rest of the room. Excess water from the infinity-edge soaking tub spills through the slatted teak shower floor into the drain.

Open Showers

Hate to feel boxed in? Consider an open shower, which has either a half wall or nothing at all to prevent water from spraying into the bathroom. In a large enough room, this usually isn't a problem, especially when the rest of the room is also tiled and easy to wipe down if necessary. You can have a step down into the shower so you won't have to worry if the drain ever backs up, but this is usually possible only in new construction where the floor can be built at varying heights. "In an existing bathroom, you can sometimes cut away portions of deep floor joists to get the right slope so you can step down into the shower, but you will need to consult with an engineer and may have to add additional floor joists to compensate," explains architect Dennis Fox.

For a modern look that's also wheelchair accessible, build a curbless shower so the bathroom floor simply extends right into the shower area. This style is also more common in new construction because a contractor will need to custom-float a large portion of the floor to ensure that it slopes toward the drain.

ABOVE LEFT Architect Kathryn Rogers designed the curbless shower in this first-floor guest bathroom to be wheelchair accessible. The handheld showerhead can slide down the metal rod for people with a lower reach.

ABOVE RIGHT A continuous sheet of ceramic mosaic tiles curves from floor to ceiling to create a walk-in shower at one end of this small bath.

OPPOSITE PAGE, LEFT A standard shower can be out-fitted for steam with a valve like this one low down on the wall. Add a simple wood bench to sit on while you're enjoying the steam; it can be folded up and out of the way for regular showers.

OPPOSITE PAGE, RIGHT This woodsy bathroom with an enclosed sauna looks as if it could be in a Swiss ski lodge. The glass door is weather-stripped so that the steamy air doesn't escape, and a two-level bench allows for multiple users.

Constructing a Steam Shower

Building a steam shower requires additional steps beyond those typical of a regular shower. "For example, it is necessary to slope the ceiling so condensation runs to the walls rather than dripping down on you."

Steam Showers and Dry Saunas

Custom and even prefabricated showers can be turned into steam showers with the addition of an electric generator that heats water and sends steam out through nozzles placed low on the shower wall. For a true spa experience, build a bench in the shower so you can lie down and enjoy the steam. You may also want to include speakers, LED lights that color the steam for relaxation or revitalization (depending on the hue you choose), fragrances, and an iPod docking station.

The steam generator will need to be installed in an accessible spot either within the bathroom or in an adjoining room. It also requires a dedicated water supply line and a dedicated 240-volt circuit. Existing shower enclosures will need to be weatherstripped to ensure that the steam doesn't escape into the bathroom, where it will cause moisture damage. And the ceiling should be tiled to protect the drywall from condensation.

If you have the space, a separate dry sauna kit that is not used for showering can be installed in the bathroom. These are constructed of clear Western red cedar and include benches for multiple users. A dry sauna may have the same electrical and plumbing requirements as previously described, or you can purchase a heat therapy room that uses radiant heat so no water line is necessary (see Resources).

Showerheads

Two showerheads and body sprays on separate controls give you the spa experience at home.

When you update your showerhead, make sure your system is safe. All new shower fittings should include a pressure-balancing valve to prevent a sudden shock of hot or cold water during a shower if someone else in the house turns on a faucet or flushes a toilet. Older showers don't have this feature, which can result in third-degree burns if your water heater is set higher than 120 degrees. It's a good idea to have one of these valves installed even if you weren't planning on renovating your shower surround.

Low-Flow Showerheads

There are two types of low-flow showerheads: aerating and laminar flow. Aerating showerheads reduce water flow by mixing air with the droplets, but they can cause the water to lose heat. If you like a really hot shower, you'll keep turning up the hot water, which means you're using more energy. Laminar-flow showerheads use individual streams of water and don't create as much steam or lose heat like aerating ones. Some manufacturers make showerheads that go as low as 1 or 1.5 gpm. Don't be afraid to try these models. With new technological advances, many feel just like a standard showerhead.

Conserving Water in a High-End Shower

While the best way to save water is to shower quickly with a 1-gpm fixture, there may be one bathroom in the house that is designed more for luxury than austerity. However, thanks to water conservation laws and manufacturers that are invested in creating a spa experience without being wasteful, there are ways to have features like multiple showerheads, body sprays, and overhead "rain" showerheads without being too wasteful. Federal law requires that showerheads emit no more than 2.5 gallons per minute (gpm), but it will not stop you from installing multiple fixtures in one shower without a way to operate them independently. So it's up to you to use these features responsibly. If you don't find a way to limit the water use in showers with multiple-head and body-spray systems, you may need to upgrade to a larger or tankless water heater and larger water supply pipes.

For example, put the second showerhead on a separate valve so that it's turned on only when the second person is there. Or for high-tech junkies, Kohler offers a digital showering system called DTV Prompt that will help you conserve resources. It allows you to select a water temperature and then pause the flow once that temperature is reached until you are

Kohler's DTV Prompt digital showering system helps you use multiple shower fixtures wisely, and it controls water temperature.

ready to step into the shower. It also sets time limits for showers (a great feature for households with teenagers), pauses the water while you shave or soap up, and controls multiple configurations (hand showers, body sprays, rain—heads) so that everything isn't running at the same time when it's not all needed at once.

Grown-Up Getaway

The freestanding tub is nicely framed by blue tile, wainscot, and a dark wood beam. A handheld showerhead allows the tub to be used for both bathing and soaking.

OPPOSITE PAGE, LEFT Dark tiles on a shower surround can make a space feel a bit confining, but it's certainly not the case in this large shower with a glass door and a top that's open to the vaulted ceiling above.

OPPOSITE PAGE, RIGHT Old-fashioned wainscot is the perfect backdrop for this console vanity, as it can be seen both above and below the marble countertop. The door leads to a separate room for the toilet.

Architect Kathryn Rogers designed this master bathroom as part of a second-story addition. In response to her client's request for as much natural light as possible, she incorporated a 12-foot-long ridge skylight that connects the master bedroom and bathroom and brightens the dramatic exposed-beam ceiling.

Blue ceramic tiles surround the generously sized shower. While there was plenty of room for multiple showerheads, the decision was made to conserve water with just one that reaches out a bit into the space. Next to the shower is a freestanding soaking tub with overhead lights for reading. The window above the tub features an etched glass design that creates privacy but allows light from the bathroom to filter into an adjoining stairwell. Two types of marble are used—tumbled tiles on the floor and a polished countertop with a distinctive pattern—adding texture and contrast to the space. Wainscot set at the same height as the shower's half wall wraps around the room, providing a visual balance to the wood ceiling.

The Elements

- **Bathtub:** Freestanding skirted tub in cast iron with vitreous porcelain interior and glossy urethane enamel exterior

- **Bathtub Faucet:** Floor-mounted with handheld showerhead and cross-handles in a polished-chrome finish

- **Shower:** Custom with handmade ceramic-tile surround; polished-chrome exterior-mount showerhead

- **Flooring:** Tumbled marble with beige grout

- **Walls:** Painted cream wainscot and pale blue walls

- **Vanity and Countertop:** Five-leg double-console vanity in polished chrome; polished Calcutta Gold marble slab

- **Sinks and Faucets:** Enameled cast-iron undermount; widespread faucet with polished-chrome finish

- **Lighting:** Recessed cans; wall sconces in polished chrome with frosted glass shades

- **Finishing Touches:** Etched glass in the window over the tub; freestanding wooden table; custom medicine cabinets with niche shelves between them

Pure Luxury

Frosted areas obscure the view through the glass shower panels in all the right places.

OPPOSITE PAGE, LEFT The striped roman shade matches the burnt orange paint and also serves a practical purpose, as this window is above the front door of the house.

OPPOSITE PAGE, RIGHT Handmade ceramic tiles with a metallic finish and abalone mosaics surround the mirrors. The vanity's rounded front mimics the barrel-vaulted ceiling.

Builder Mark De Mattei pulled out all the stops on this master bathroom. "I wanted something completely different that hadn't been done before, which is challenging, especially when the existing home is traditional. So to mix an edgy design into this traditional home, I kept it elegant but fun," Mark says.

The first thing you see upon opening two frosted glass doors is the deck-mounted tub, sitting right in the center of the room under a barrel-vaulted ceiling. In the foreground is an ornate mosaic marble "rug" that's reflected in three beveled mirrors set in the tub deck. Hanging above appears to be a tray of white candles, but it's actually an electric light controlled by a dimmer switch,

allowing for a soft, faux-candlelight glow that's perfect for evening soaks.

Two rooms on either side of the tub are outfitted with heavy glass shower doors, but only one is a shower—the other creates a semi-private area for the toilet. The glass panel above the shower door swivels open to allow steam to escape. When closed, the shower turns into a tightly sealed steam room.

The Elements

- **Bathtub and Faucet:** Deck-mounted limestone surround; widespread brushed-nickel faucet with glass handles and retractable handheld showerhead

- **Shower:** Custom steam shower with bench, multiple showerheads, and handheld showerhead

- **Flooring:** Crema Marfil honed marble

- **Walls:** Crema Marfil honed marble; ceramic and mosaic tile; paint

- **Vanity:** Custom face-frame with glazed crackle painted finish

- **Countertop:** Limestone slab

- **Sink:** Undermount in hammered nickel

- **Sink Faucet:** Widespread with brushed-nickel finish and glass handles

- **Toilet:** One-piece, 1.6 gpf

- **Lighting:** Recessed cans; wall sconces; spotlights; dimmable candelabra

- **Finishing Touches:** Soft roman shades; framed wall mirrors; polished-nickel knobs and pulls; frosted glass designs; crown molding

Chapter 6

Lighting, Heating, and Ventilation

Nobody wants a stale, moldy, smelly bathroom, but that's what you'll eventually have if the room isn't properly ventilated. Far from a mere technicality, good ventilation is a crucial part of your new or remodeled bathroom. We'll help you sort through the lighting choices and come up with an energy-efficient plan that works for your space. Take this opportunity to add windows or skylights if you can, and consider new or additional heat sources, such as in-floor radiant heat, so your bare feet will never be cold.

Fresh air flows into this bathing nook, thanks to a wall of awning-style windows. Recessed spots and a decorative chandelier keep the lighting scheme mellow at night.

Creating a Lighting Plan

Lights installed behind the mirror wash the walls with soft illumination. Spotlights above offer task lighting for the vanity area.

Lighting design is an art. If you already have an architect or interior designer working on your bathroom remodel, he or she will be able to design a lighting plan for you that takes into account natural light sources, reflectivity, and any light loss or gain from various colored materials and surfaces in the room. If not, consider hiring a professional lighting designer to figure out the best combination of fixtures and bulbs for a complicated space. You may also get some valuable advice from showroom personnel at a retail lighting store.

Types of Light

Designers use the following terminology to describe the four categories of lighting:

AMBIENT LIGHTING provides general, indirect illumination. In a very small bathroom or half bath, you may not need more light than the fixtures installed around the mirror, in which case those task lights would also be supplying ambient light for the room. In larger bathrooms, ceiling fixtures or wall sconces can be placed in various spots to light up the entire space.

TASK LIGHTING comes from fixtures that direct focused light for a particular activity. Lights around a bathroom mirror are task lights, as are any fixtures placed next to the toilet or tub for reading, or at a makeup table.

ACCENT LIGHTING provides drama in a room. Small, bright lights are focused on a particular object, such as an above-counter stone sink, or an architectural feature like a wall niche, to draw the eye to them. Different fixtures and bulbs provide varying beam widths to match the size of the object you're highlighting.

DECORATIVE LIGHTING adds to the decor of the room but doesn't add much illumination. Candles fall into this category as well.

This funky fixture made of lime fabric wasn't designed for a bathroom, but it adds some style to a half bath where there's no steam to damage it.

INTERIOR DESIGNER
TERRELL GOEKE ON

Combining Types of Fixtures

A good designer will help you create a plan that involves ambient, task, accent, and decorative light sources. "I like to put a variety of recessed lights, sconces, pendants, and cabinet lights in the bathrooms I design."

Lighting a Bathroom

The mirror above the vanity is the most critical area to light. This is where people will be fixing their hair, shaving, inspecting their faces for wrinkles, and applying makeup, so it's important that the light be as even and natural as possible.

Cross light, the kind of light you'll get from having wall sconces or vertical tube lights on both sides of the mirror, is the preferred goal around the vanity. Architect Dennis Fox says that when you put a light above the mirror or, worse yet, on the ceiling, you get the opposite effect from that of holding a flashlight under your chin. "Theater dressing rooms have exposed lightbulbs all the way around the mirrors, which gives the cross-light effect you want when you're putting on makeup," he explains.

Recessed ceiling fixtures are a popular way to bring ambient light into the bathroom. Just make sure you buy waterproof recessed cans. The size of the can and the bulb wattage will dictate how far apart the fixtures should be placed in the room. And don't forget to plan for any lights needed in separate areas such as the shower and toilet stalls.

TOP RIGHT Lighting catalogs are full of simple task fixtures like these meant to flank the vanity. They come in different metal finishes so you can select something that works with your faucets and showerhead.

BOTTOM RIGHT Tall ceilings beg for artistic hanging fixtures. This chandelier is the cherry on top of an elegant mosaic-faced tub and custom round window.

ARCHITECT
DENNIS FOX ON

Dimmer Switches

Always put your bathroom lights on dimmer switches. "That way you can take a relaxing bath without bright lights blaring, and you can keep the lights dim when you use the bathroom in the middle of the night. Put a dimmer switch on the wall sconces around your vanity as well, so you can turn those lights up all the way when applying makeup, and use softer light for general illumination."

In a bathroom with plenty of natural light, you can opt for fixtures with less wattage. This hanging lamp provides mood lighting during evening soaks.

The right bulbs will give your bathroom a warm, radiant glow.

Choosing Lightbulbs

The fixtures you choose will depend on the type of light you want them to provide, as well as the style of the room. But the bulb you put in the fixture is just as important as the fixture itself. The bulb is what creates either warm or bright light, and it can even add heat to the room.

In an effort to increase energy efficiency, most cities require that a certain percentage of the wattage in your bathroom come from compact fluorescent lightbulbs (CFLs) or light-emitting diodes (LED). If you are not remodeling and still using incandescent bulbs, consider adding an occupancy sensor. "So energy is saved either through higher-efficacy lighting or sensors that turn off lighting when the bath is unoccupied," says architect David Gast.

Wiring the lighting fixtures so that they're controlled by dimmer switches is a nice touch and allows a lot more flexibility. Once hard to find, dimmable CFLs that screw into standard fixtures are now widely available.

INCANDESCENT lightbulbs have been around since 1878. They are inexpensive and emit a warm light, but they aren't energy efficient. A federal phase-out of incandescent bulbs in the United States began with 100-watt bulbs in 2012 and will continue with 40- and 60-watt bulbs beginning in 2014. So replace any incandescent bulbs you have left as soon as possible to save energy and money.

COMPACT FLUORESCENT lightbulbs (CFLs) provide more light per watt than incandescent or halogen bulbs, yet they use about 75 percent less energy and release a negligible amount of heat. If every American household replaced just one incandescent bulb with a CFL, it would reduce greenhouse gases equivalent to the emissions that nearly 800,000 cars emit each year. CFLs can last up to 10 times as long as incandescent bulbs. Most CFLs screw into fixtures made for incandescent bulbs, but you can also purchase fixtures that work only with special 2- or 4-pin fluorescent bulbs.

COMPACT FLUORESCENTS

HALOGENS

4-PIN FLUORESCENT

2-PIN FLUORESCENT

HALOGEN lightbulbs produce a whiter, brighter beam than other bulbs and are most often used for accent lighting. They do get very hot, which is why they can be used only in fixtures that are designed for them. You may find low-voltage pendants and downlights that take special forms of halogen bulbs called MR16 or MR11. These tiny bulbs come in a range of beam widths, from narrow to wide flood.

LIGHT-EMITTING DIODE (LED) bulbs use 90 percent less energy than incandescent lightbulbs, last even longer than CFLs, and stay cool enough to touch. Some LED bulbs can screw into standard household light sockets, though they are more commonly built into specialty decorative light fixtures.

INCANDESCENTS

Natural Light

A breathtaking
combination of
windows—including
clerestories on top,
a fixed outside corner,
and a large awning-
style—illuminate this
large bathroom and
offer views of the
treetops beyond.

Windows and skylights not only make a bathroom brighter, they also create an open feel and help give the room a connection to nature. If your bathroom has at least one exterior wall, hire an architect or builder to figure out how you can add one or more windows. Look for ways to bring natural light in through skylights if the bathroom is on the top floor. Interior bathrooms that don't share any exterior walls and are on lower floors can also get natural light through Solatubes® (see page 163) or through glass blocks in interior walls leading to rooms that do.

Windows

For clients who are sensitive to being viewed from outside while in the bathroom, architect David Gast recommends high windows. "They provide natural light and ventilation and allow use of the wall space below while providing privacy." Make sure wood windows are given a couple of coats of marine-grade urethane finish to protect them from the moisture in the bathroom, and reapply it regularly. Vinyl windows will be easiest to maintain, but metal windows should be kept out of the bathroom, as they can rust in moist environments. If possible, choose the same style and finish as you have elsewhere in the house.

While there are ways to provide privacy without covering windows with blinds or shades (see box at right), there's also a high-tech solution that architect Beth Gensemer is a fan of. "With the flip of a switch, SwitchLite Privacy Glass goes from clear to translucent, so you get daylight when you want it and privacy when you need it," she explains.

Maintain privacy without giving up natural light by ordering lower windowpanes with translucent finishes.

INTERIOR DESIGNER
HEIDI PRIBELL ON

Decorative Glass Finishes

Consider ordering custom glass for your bathroom windows to prevent people from being able to see through them from the outside and to add a decorative feature to the room as well. "I like to use two types of frosted glass in a harlequin pattern so you can get natural light but still have some privacy." Glass artists can create practically any design imaginable to provide various levels of obscurity, including custom frosted scenes that mimic your garden, stained glass in the colors of your choice, or wavy finishes.

Skylights

There's nothing quite like soaking in the tub while gazing up at a full moon or watching the sun rising or setting. You'll get the most out of a bathroom skylight if you place it properly. "Don't just put a skylight in the middle of a room. Locate it over something—an object, a task—reinforcing that object," explains architect Dennis Fox. "Used improperly, a skylight can look like just a hole in the ceiling. Used properly, it can serve an architectural function."

An operable skylight over a shower not only brings in natural light but acts like a chimney to reduce steam in the room. Try to avoid installing a skylight directly over a vanity, though, as the overhead light it provides can be unwelcome at certain times of the day if you're applying makeup.

Wherever you live, be sure to have the skylight installed by an experienced professional to avoid air and water leaks. In some climates, however, skylights are more trouble than they're worth. "In the Midwest, we have maintenance issues generated from snow and ice, so people tend to shy away from skylights," says interior designer Terrell Goeke. "Plus they're harder to cover, so during the summer they let a lot of heat into the bathroom. I'm more prone to include windows with motorized window treatments to control the light," he says.

Other Daylighting Options

Aside from windows and skylights, there are other creative ways to add natural light to a bathroom. Tubular daylighting devices are inexpensive and easy to install. A relatively small

hole is cut into the roof, and a dome equipped with reflectors is inserted. A series of tubes coated with a reflective material lead from the dome to the room, ending in a ceiling-mounted fixture that looks much like a recessed electric light. Architect Anne Laird-Blanton prefers the Energy Star–rated Solatube® system. "I designed an interior bath on the lower floor with no natural light, and we used a Solatube that came in from two stories above with great results," she says.

Glass blocks can be installed in both interior and exterior walls to bring more light into a room. They can be grouped together or placed randomly across a wall, and the thick glass does a good job of obscuring what's on the other side.

OPPOSITE PAGE, LEFT High up in a cathedral ceiling, this skylight bounces large amounts of light across the walls and creates a bright feeling in a room with a dark slate floor and stained wood vanities.

OPPOSITE PAGE, RIGHT To get some natural light into an adjoining room with no windows, the designer of this bathroom replaced the drywall in the shower with a second glass panel. The book-shelves in the living space provide some privacy but still allow light through.

ABOVE LEFT Using glass blocks on an outside wall will wash the room in natural light and create interesting patterns as the sun progresses throughout the day.

ABOVE RIGHT Floor-to-ceiling translucent glass blocks allow light into the tub and shower area. Square glass mosaics and two square wall-mount sinks were chosen to complement the wall design.

Ventilation

Open showers with no doors require powerful bathroom fans installed nearby to prevent the moisture from damaging the bathroom walls or adjoining rooms.

Having an operable window or skylight in a bathroom can help reduce steam, but it's no substitute for a bathroom fan. If you don't already have one, a fan should be installed during the remodel process, even if your city code doesn't require one. It will keep your new finishes and fixtures from being damaged by excess moisture, which can lead to mold and mildew.

Choosing a Bathroom Fan

The most common bathroom fans are mounted in the ceiling or wall and suck moist air through ductwork vented through the roof or an exterior wall. These fans come as one unit that includes the motor and either a light fixture (shown above right) or just a grille that's visible in the bathroom itself (shown above left). Some even have heaters. A more powerful and expensive option is an in-line remote fan that's installed on the roof or in the attic and is attached to one or more inlets in one or more bathrooms (see page 166).

The Home Ventilating Institute (HVI) has a certified rating program that tests ventilation products, including bathroom fans, and its symbol on a box certifies that the product moves as much air as it claims to. The HVI recommends that a bathroom fan be capable of exchanging the air in a room at least 8 times per hour. So it's important to figure out how powerful a fan you need before going shopping for one. To do this, multiply the length of your bathroom by the width and height and then by the number 8 (the number of air exchanges per hour). Convert that number from hours to minutes by dividing by 60 and you'll get the right cubic feet per minute, or CFM, rating for your room. For example, if your room is 8 feet long by 7 feet wide and has an 8-foot-high ceiling, the equation would be: $8 \times 7 \times 8 \times 8 = 3{,}584$, which divided by 60 equals 59.73, so you'd need a 60 CFM fan.

The minimum recommended CFM rating for a bathroom fan is 50, but there are exceptions. If your bathroom has separate rooms for the toilet, bath, and shower area, each of those areas should have its own 50 CFM fan. This holds true even if these areas share one room but the entire space is larger than 100 square feet. Jetted tubs and steam showers require even higher CFM-rated fans. And special circumstances such as cathedral ceilings and how many twists and turns the ductwork needs to make also affect the fan's efficiency. Your architect or builder will be able to help you determine the best fan or system for your situation.

NOISE is another concern with bathroom fans. The amount of noise a fan generates is measured in sones; look for the sone rating on the fan's box. The quietest fans on the market have a rating of 0.5 sones and will barely be noticeable. But most people are happy with up to 1.5 sones. Home improvement centers often have fans mounted on a display so you can turn them on and hear the sound they make before purchasing.

THE RIGHT LOCATION for the fan depends on your situation. When a bathroom fan includes a light, most people put it in the center of the room. But architect Beth Gensemer recommends putting the fan close to the shower. "That way, more steam will get sucked into the fan before it fogs up the mirror," she says.

Timers and Sensors

The Home Ventilating Institute recommends that you run the bathroom fan for 20 minutes after a shower or bath to completely clear the room of moist air. When you have a particularly loud fan, it can be tempting to turn it off earlier than that. Some people might leave the fan on for hours, wasting electricity, if they go to another part of the house and can't hear that it's still on. To reduce energy consumption and ensure that the bathroom is being adequately dried, put your bathroom fan on a sensor or timer.

A timer switch can be set to turn off after a certain amount of time—usually there's a choice of 10, 20, 30, or 60 minutes. You can also choose a humidity-sensing switch, which will turn the fan on once the room reaches a certain level of humidity and turn it off when the level is back to normal. This is a great option for people who may not remember to turn the fan on at all.

TOP In this bathroom, ventilation was turned into a design feature. Wires attached to the ceiling hold up a large glass panel surrounded by metal trim, which seems to hover over the shower area. The vent pipe, usually hidden in the ceiling, is exposed and painted orange.

BOTTOM Bathroom fans are commonly installed just outside the shower area to catch steamy air at the source.

BUILDER MARK DE MATTEI ON

Multiple-Inlet Fans

While every bathroom needs a fan, sometimes one just isn't enough. "For large bathrooms, and particularly those that have a steam shower, I suggest using a Fantech system with multiple inlets to move larger amounts of air. The fan itself is mounted away from the bathroom and connected via ductwork to each inlet, which is an unobtrusive ceiling grille with or without a dimmable halogen light."

When you have a lot of wood in your bathroom, getting the steam out quickly is even more important. An open window that spans the shower and tub areas assists the ceiling fan.

Heating the Bath

These toe-kick heaters are barely noticeable, as the vents are recessed under the vanities. In this bathroom addition, using toe-kick heaters was less expensive than extending the existing forced-air system.

RIGHT If possible, install a forced-air register low on the wall when extending the system so the heat will rise as it fills the room. When the register is placed high up on a wall, the heat takes a little longer to work its way down.

The bathroom you're remodeling probably already has a heat source. It could be part of a ducted forced-air system or have an existing radiator. While it's essential to have some form of heat in the bathroom, warmer climates will need less of it than colder ones. For some, an electric radiant-heat mat (see page 170) that takes the chill off a cold tile floor is really all that's needed.

Choosing a Heating System

If you are building a new bathroom or want to change what you have as part of a remodel, you will be in the market for a new heating system. The one that works for you will depend on many factors, including the location of the bathroom in the house. When an existing forced-air system can't be extended to the new bathroom because of accessibility issues, you'll need to install a supplemental heat system.

HEAT LAMPS can be installed in the ceiling or upper wall, alone or in conjunction with a ventilation fan. In small bathrooms, these can be effective enough, although you'll get the most heat when you're standing directly underneath the lamp, and when you get too hot, you usually can't turn it down, just on or off. Heaters that blow hot air into the bathroom will keep the space from getting too steamy, as they raise the temperature in the room closer to that of the hot water.

TOE-KICK HEATERS fit in the toe-kick area underneath standard vanities. These are similar to stand-alone space heaters, except that they don't take up any extra floor space. Hot-water pipes or electricity heats air, and a fan blows it out into the room. Some people find these heaters annoying because your ankles can get hot if you're standing in front of the vanity for a long period. "Because toe-kick heaters warm up a space rapidly, putting it on a timer so that it turns on before you wake up may not be necessary," says architect David Gast.

TOP Nuheat® radiant mats are popular for remodels because you can install them easily and inexpensively between the subfloor and the finished floor without raising its height to a problematic level.

BOTTOM Hydronic radiant heat systems look like this. Hot water runs through the tubes that are installed over (or under) the subfloor. The heat rises through the finished floor, warming cold tiles or concrete while also heating the room.

RADIANT HEAT comes up through the finished floor. With radiant heat, there is no hot air blowing, which is helpful for people with allergies. The systems also make no noise, and there are no vents to work around.

An inexpensive and popular solution for cold bathroom floors is electric radiant-heat mats, which are mortared in place over the subfloor (or some types of existing finished floors) and then covered with a new floor. Be sure to select a flooring material that can handle being heated and cooled repeatedly, such as ceramic tile. Some types of stone don't do as well with this type of heat as others (see page 40), and most varieties of wood floors and resilient flooring such as cork and linoleum aren't recommended for this system either. Because the mats are so thin, they don't add much to the height of the floor. Architect Anne Laird-Blanton is a fan of Nuheat® mats and recommends this system to most of her clients. "These are only expensive if you get into customized mat sizes. If you can work with standard-sized mats, this system is very reasonable in price," she says.

Homeowners can lay the mats themselves if they want to, but the final connections should be made by a licensed electrician. Most systems come with a timer that turns the heat on well before you wake up so the floor is warm when you walk into the bathroom for your early-morning shower. Because heat rises, warmth from the floor will radiate into the room's air, and in temperate climates, this may be all the heat you need. In cooler climates, heat mats can supplement another system. Aside from radiant-heat mats, there are electric cable systems that can be embedded in a poured concrete subfloor or finished floor, or covered with mortar and tile. This option is less expensive than mats if you plan to heat the whole house this way.

Hydronic radiant heat is considered the king of heat systems, and it is more effective and energy efficient than installing electric radiant heat throughout an entire home. In a remodel, tubes are attached to the underside of your subfloor (accessed from the crawl space or basement). Hot water runs through the tubes, heating up the subfloor and, in turn, the finished floor and the air in the room. Layers of insulation under the tubes keep the heat from migrating down into the ground. In new construction, the tubes are generally installed before a poured concrete subfloor. Most hydronic radiant-heat systems run throughout a whole house rather than in just one room. They must be installed by a professional and will require either a boiler or a tankless water heater to handle the extra hot-water demands.

ARCHITECT ANNE LAIRD-BLANTON ON

Energy Usage

Electric radiant-heat mats can be expensive to run if you leave them on all the time at a low level so the floor never gets cold. "But they can also save energy in a house with a forced-air system because you don't have to turn on the heat in the whole house just to warm up the bathroom." A hydronic radiant-heat system can be used in the same way as long as it is zoned so that each room can be controlled separately.

This concrete floor was colored with a non-toxic soy-based stain and is kept warm by the hydronic heat system installed underneath.

RADIATORS can be found as long and narrow fixtures that run across the baseboard, stand-alone cast-iron fixtures in older homes, or modern sculpture-like systems that are available in a variety of colors, shapes, and sizes. For hydronic radiators, a boiler heats the water, which circulates through pipes or tubes to the radiator and warms up the room. In steam systems, the boiler turns water into steam, which rises through pipes and is released into the room, then condenses back into water and returns to the boiler. There are also electric radiators, which require a dedicated electrical circuit.

As part of a bathroom remodel, cast-iron radiators can be given a coat of paint, replaced with another vintage radiator, or surrounded by a radiator cover that doesn't hinder the heat from reaching the room but hides a style of fixture that may not work with the new look you're going for.

TOWEL WARMERS work as a heat source only in bathrooms that don't need much heat. If you live in a temperate climate and have a warm floor, such as linoleum or cork, a towel warmer might do the trick. In addition to heating the room a little bit, towel warmers will dry your wet towels much faster, keeping them smelling fresh longer. They can be powered by either electricity or hot water.

TOP RIGHT Hydronic radiators have decorative panels that can coordinate with other fixtures in the bathroom.

BOTTOM RIGHT This new radiator in stainless steel mimics the look of an old-fashioned model. Installing it below the countertop in lieu of cabinetry saves floor space and makes the room feel larger, although storage space is lost.

OPPOSITE PAGE, TOP LEFT Some people think of their old-fashioned cast-iron radiators as an attractive period feature in a vintage bathroom; others may want to hide them behind covers or free-standing furniture.

OPPOSITE PAGE, TOP RIGHT A long, gray baseboard radiator extends under two wall-mounted sinks. The bath mat helps to keep bare feet warm and also protects the hardwood floor.

OPPOSITE PAGE, BOTTOM LEFT A polished chrome radiator matches the finish of the plumbing fixtures in a bathroom with a sleek wall-mounted glass sink.

OPPOSITE PAGE, BOTTOM RIGHT Radiators are now available in a range of modern styles, including this one with horizontal slats. A couple of slats were removed so that the radiator could double as a towel warmer.

Bright and Airy

Back-to-back floating vanities give each person his or her own space. Deep, wide wall-mounted sinks make a design statement, and setting them on a solid-surface countertop that connects on the far side means that some toiletries can be more easily shared.

OPPOSITE PAGE The glass panel above the shower door can be closed when the steam shower is in use, or opened to let steam escape.

This master bath was built as part of a top-floor addition to a 1950s ranch house. The well-traveled homeowners asked architect Anne Laird-Blanton to create a contemporary hotel-spa feeling using a limited amount of square footage. Anne was able to squeeze two vanities into the narrow room by incorporating a dividing wall that allows them to face each other and still have their own mirrored medicine cabinets.

Anne put windows on two sides of the room to flood it with natural light and to take advantage of the stunning views of nearby mountains. The windows are operable, allowing for cross-ventilation that makes the room more comfortable and also assists the bathroom fans.

Unique light fixtures are made of die-cut birch veneer that picks up on the color and texture of the floating vanities and tub surround. When lit, the lights have a warm orange glow. Two large basket drum pendants hang from the ceiling, and a wall sconce version in the same design softly illuminates the separate toilet alcove. Task lighting is built into the mirrors in the form of fluorescent tubes.

Terrazzo floor tiles speckled with shards of recycled glass in shades of orange pick up on the color of the light fixtures. Completing the spa bath are a glass and marble-tiled steam shower and speakers that provide background music during a soak in the tub.

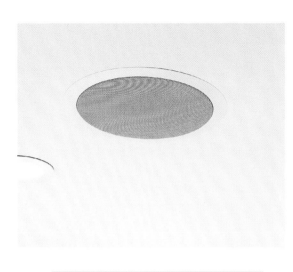

The Elements

- **Lighting:** Recessed; ceiling fixture and wall sconce made of birch veneer; fluorescent lights around vanity mirrors

- **Ventilation:** Operable windows; two fans

- **Flooring:** Terrazzo with orange glass

- **Walls:** White and blue paint

- **Vanities:** Custom floating frameless in maple

- **Countertops:** Solid surface

- **Sinks:** Wall-mounted porcelain

- **Sink Faucets:** Wall-mounted in polished chrome

- **Bathtub:** Deck-mounted jetted tub with polished-chrome side-mount faucet; solid-surface deck and maple surround

- **Shower:** Steam shower with glass subway and Carrera marble tiles; dual showerheads; bench; glass doors

- **Toilet:** One-piece, 1.6 gpf

- **Finishing Touches:** Mirrored medicine cabinets; polished chrome pulls and towel bars

Open windows bring in plenty of fresh air and light. On one side of the house, they were installed above shoulder height for privacy, but this was not an issue with the large window over the tub, as it looks out over open land.

LEFT Low-profile speakers set into the ceiling allow the homeowners to listen to music while relaxing in their spa bath.

OPPOSITE PAGE Deep blue walls envelop you in this narrow alcove that provides just enough privacy, even without a door.

Southern Hospitality

Styled almost like a living room, this is a bathroom that you can spend hours in quite comfortably.

Architect Bill Ingram designed this new master bath as an addition to a 1920s English Colonial house in Birmingham, Alabama. "It's a long and narrow lot, and although the floor-to-ceiling bay window matches others on the outside of the house, it really didn't suit the privacy needs for a bathroom," he said. The bay window was, however, an ideal backdrop for a freestanding bathtub, as it allowed the homeowner to gaze up at the sky while soaking. So Bill added a period-perfect upholstered floor screen with metal grommets, as well as a soft roman shade at the top of the window for extra privacy when needed.

The freestanding cabinet to the right of the tub serves as a room divider between the bathroom and an exercise space. "Cabinet doors open on both sides, and the television is on a swivel stand so you can watch it either in the exercise room or the bathroom," Bill explains.

The Elements

- **Lighting:** Wall sconces in oil-rubbed bronze with cream shades

- **Flooring:** Reclaimed oak in random widths

- **Walls:** Painted off-white

- **Vanities:** Custom-painted face-frame with raised diamond-shaped door panels; matching freestanding cabinet

- **Countertops:** Honed limestone slabs

- **Sinks:** Enameled cast-iron undermounts

- **Sink Faucets:** Widespread goosenecks with polished-nickel finish

- **Bathtub:** Freestanding vintage-style in enameled cast iron

- **Bathtub Faucet:** Floor-mounted with handheld showerhead in a polished-nickel finish

- **Finishing Touches:** Polished-nickel soap holders; tub caddy; framed mirrors; soft roman shades; upholstered floor screen; handwoven rug; leather sling-back chair; plants

Chapter 7

Finishing Touches

Turning a well-designed and appointed space into one that's truly your own calls for finishing touches such as mirrors, window coverings that provide privacy and style, rods and hooks to hold plush new towels, bath and shower caddies to keep bottles off the edge of the tub or floor of the shower, and much more. If you decided on neutrals for the walls and floor, use these accessories to add color and incorporate creature comforts that will make it even harder to leave your beautiful new bathroom.

Dress up your bathroom with an ornate mirror, pretty waste basket, stylish cabinet hardware, and coordinating towels.

Medicine Cabinets

In most small bathrooms, installing a medicine cabinet behind the vanity mirror is a standard way to get some extra storage space. Large bathrooms don't always need a traditional medicine cabinet. In these cases, you can get more creative with the mirror.

Architect Dennis Fox prefers to use custom-made wooden medicine cabinets. "Instead of buying a metal medicine cabinet—which makes a horrible noise when you open and close it and will rust over time—ask a custom cabinetmaker to build a wooden cabinet for you," he explains. "You'll get a larger medicine cabinet, and it will close quietly."

Some medicine cabinets are equipped with a light that turns on when the door opens or with a receptacle for plugging in your electric toothbrush. You'll need to plan for these well in advance so that the electrician can bring the wires to the right spot while the walls are still open.

ARCHITECT
KATHRYN ROGERS ON

Medicine Cabinet Shelves

A common problem with the shelves in medicine cabinets is that over time they get dirty and sticky from spilled toiletries. People prefer the clean look of glass shelves, but they are hard to maintain. The solution? Mirrored shelves. "To keep the shelves looking clean, use mirror shelves with a polished edge instead of glass so you don't see the crud under the bottles."

ABOVE A plain white medicine cabinet can be dressed up with crown and base molding. In this bathroom, the molding profiles were chosen to coordinate with the surrounding capped wainscot wall.

OPPOSITE PAGE Set into a wall niche, this tall medicine cabinet offers plenty of closed storage and makes the room brighter by reflecting light from the window.

Mirrors

Mirrors can be as bold or as understated as you like. Here, a wreath of lacquered willow branches surrounds a tall oval mirror over this simple wall-hung sink.

The bathroom mirror can be a small and simple affair or a grand statement of style. Some people prefer the clean and simple lines of an unframed mirror, while others turn the mirror into a piece of art. Architect Anne Laird-Blanton suggests taking a mirror in the size you want to a custom frame shop to create something unique.

Architect Beth Gensemer prefers frameless mirrors that extend from the countertop to about 7 feet above the floor and the full length of the vanity. Large mirrors open up the room, and they reflect more light. Plus, they give you a lot of bang for your buck—they're not expensive if you don't frame them. "But I don't like to see outlets in the mirror or on the countertop, where they will reflect in the mirror, so I always have at least one receptacle inside the vanity. That way you can store your electric toothbrush and your hair dryer in the vanity and keep them plugged in, but they aren't cluttering up the countertop," she says. If you have full-length mirrors, you can still put a medicine cabinet behind them; just install a separate piece of mirror with a touch-latch that you push to open the door. "That way, you can have a custom-sized medicine cabinet that's flush with the surrounding mirrors. Just make sure that the mirror's seams are placed away from where you'll normally stand," Beth explains.

Specialty mirrors include tilted versions that "float" in front of the wall and have more of a furniture look than standard bathroom mirrors. Magnifying mirrors—handy for applying makeup or shaving—need blocking in the walls to support their weight, and electrical power if they have built-in lights. Vanity mirrors that come with lights on either side will also need electrical power, so plan for these while the electrician is doing the rough-in work.

LEFT A magnifying mirror on a movable arched rod resembles the earth orbiting the sun.

ABOVE If you want to combine several mirrors in the bathroom, opt for ones that have the same finish for a more unified design.

TOP LEFT This angular vintage mirror offset from the sink makes for a quirky bath design when combined with a modern concrete counter and painted wood-paneled wall.

TOP RIGHT Bronze accents on this ornate mirror coordinate with the sink and faucet below. The countertop was kept neutral so that the mirror could take center stage.

RIGHT Pieces of beveled mirror are set at a diagonal and combined into one large area, creating a pattern where there normally wouldn't be one.

OPPOSITE PAGE This mirror was built into the wall that separates the shower from the vanity. A deep ledge was incorporated for a bit of small toiletry storage.

INTERIOR DESIGNER
HEIDI PRIBELL ON

Powder Room Mirrors

In a shared bathroom or a master bath, it's tempting to combine the medicine cabinet with the mirror to get some extra storage space. "But in a powder room, the mirror is a great opportunity to get glamorous and use something more decorative."

Window Coverings

E ven if you live in a secluded area with plenty of space between the houses, chances are you will need some kind of window covering in your bathroom (unless you chose a glass finish that provides privacy; see page 163). Besides keeping you hidden from the world while you are in the buff, window coverings keep heat from escaping, and they add to the overall style of the room.

Soft Window Treatments

Fabric window treatments provide a softer look in the bathroom. Shades can have flat or billowy folds and generally hang within the window frame. Architect Bill Ingram likes to use soft roman shades to add color and drama to the bathrooms he designs. Curtains can cover the bottom half of a window, or the fabric can hang from the top of the window and end in a pool on the floor. Half baths that won't get too steamy are better for large amounts of expensive fabrics that must be dry-cleaned. Check the transparency of the fabric you're interested in, and add lining to the back if you require more privacy.

Hard Window Treatments

Blinds and shutters allow you to let some light into the room while also blocking off the view from outside when tilted slightly up or down. For large windows, design shutters in sections so you can close the ones on the bottom and keep the top sections open. Install blinds that can move up and down on the window to cover whatever portion is necessary, instead of ones that can operate only from the top down. Be sure that wooden blinds and shutters are painted and sealed so that they won't suffer any moisture damage or have expansion and contraction issues.

ABOVE Dramatic arched windows surround an alcove for a jetted tub. These narrow slatted shutters have a more period look than wide plantation shutters do.

OPPOSITE PAGE Soft roman shades in a punchy pattern are the focal point of this cheerful blue bathroom. If you need more privacy but want to let the sunlight in, order your shades "top down, bottom up" so you have the option of lowering the fabric at the top of the window and keeping the bottom portion drawn.

Accessories

The floor and wall finishes and the fixtures you choose will create the overall style of your bathroom, and that style can be reinforced or turned up a notch with the accessories you add once the room is complete.

For interior designer Heidi Pribell, decorating the bathroom is like putting the icing on the cake. "When I'm designing an Edwardian bathroom, it's the creature comforts that make it warm, personalized, and hospitable. English bathrooms are decorated and treated more like living spaces than lavatories. I draw inspiration from them to make bathrooms more compatible with dressing areas. I think there's a certain grandeur in that," she says.

TOWELS can be much more than a utilitarian item for drying off. Pick a color or group of colors that either blend with or enhance the colors you chose for the walls and floor. White towels in a room with cream-colored walls and gray and white marble floors and counters have the refined elegance of a five-star hotel bath, while putting bright green towels in the same room gives it a punchy, youthful flair.

There are many styles and sizes of towel bars. The safest bet is to match the finish with that of your sink and shower fixtures, though it's certainly not a rule. Pick a towel bar that fits in the space you have and will hold as many towels as you need. Architect Beth Gensemer recommends adding blocking to the wall studs when the drywall is off, at the beginning of the project, where you plan to install the towel bar. "There's nothing worse than a wobbly towel bar in a new bathroom," she says.

Towel warmers dry wet towels faster, making them smell fresher and last longer. Plus they give your towels that just-out-of-the-dryer feeling that can't be beat on a cold day. If you want a towel warmer, it's best to plan for one at the start so the electrician can bring power to the right spot while roughing in wires for other fixtures. Otherwise you'll have to deal with a power cord, which can look sloppy.

ABOVE LEFT You may have to search a bit, but it's possible to find unique designs such as this artistic towel holder that was chosen to coordinate with the lantern-style light fixture.

ABOVE RIGHT In a rustic bath where shiny chrome fixtures would look out of place, a short wooden ladder offers a place to hang linens.

OPPOSITE PAGE One advantage to having an extra-wide shower is that you can install a towel bar inside it. The polished chrome finish and style match those of the shower fixtures.

CANDLES add romance and elegance to the bath. Put a grouping of softly scented candles around the tub to perfume the air and provide a warm glow during evening soaks.

SHOWER CURTAINS are often an afterthought picked up at the drugstore when you're out doing other errands, but a carefully chosen one can enhance the style of the bathroom. Fabric shower curtains are available in hundreds of colors and patterns. Pair them with a waterproof liner to protect them from getting soaked. There are also printed shower curtains made of materials that can handle direct contact with water. You can even get creative with the curtain rings, which come in various metal finishes and designs.

HOUSEPLANTS bring nature indoors, and some help remove toxins from the air you breathe. Choose varieties that will thrive in the steamy environment of the bathroom. Also keep flower vases in guest baths and half baths and fill them with fresh-cut flowers. The sight of them will make you smile every time you enter the room.

BATH MATS AND RUGS give you something soft and secure to step onto when getting out of the tub or stepping out of the shower. Make sure they have a slip-resistant rubber backing. They also take the chill off a cold tile or stone floor, and they protect wood floors from splashes. Bath mats tend to get heavy use and should be machine washable. Rugs placed in front of a vanity or away from frequent splashes can be kept clean with regular vacuuming and by being aired out on a clothesline a couple of times a year.

FAR LEFT, TOP Votive candles on tall metal pillars accent a restored claw-foot tub.

FAR LEFT, BOTTOM A leafy botanical print adds a soft touch to this brick-walled shower.

LEFT A pale gray rug takes the chill off four-inch terra-cotta floor tiles in this kids' bath.

OPPOSITE PAGE Consider hanging a living wall of succulents in a bath that gets plenty of natural light.

LEFT Standing racks allow soap to dry faster and last longer. Dishes with solid sides and bottoms are best for holding decorative guest soaps.

RIGHT Place a decorative cup filled with toothbrushes in the guest bath.

SOAP AND TOOTHBRUSH HOLDERS aren't a necessity—these items certainly can and often do just sit on the edge of the sink—but they will help create a finished and orderly look in the bathroom. Most manufacturers offer matching finishes for soap, toothbrush, and cup holders in varying styles, from hard-edged and modern to gilded and traditional. You can also fill glass canisters or vases with soaps and other bath accessories.

BATH AND SHOWER CADDIES keep soaps and shampoo off the floor and within arm's reach. In a freestanding tub, the bath caddy serves a practical purpose because there is no tub deck on which to set toiletries. But it can also be used to hold up a book while you soak in the tub, or serve a purely decorative function by looking picture perfect on a restored claw-foot. Be sure to buy caddies made of chrome, as metal-plated versions will rust over time.

A TELEVISION in the bathroom must be planned for, as you'll need to wire for it and possibly add blocking to the wall studs to support the extra weight while the walls are still open. An even more high-tech solution is to put a television inside a special mirror so that when the TV is off you can't see it at all, but when it's on, the picture magically appears. This arrangement is often used in a mirrored tub surround or in the middle of a double vanity. Installing electrical equipment behind a wall is obviously more complicated, especially if there are problems with the equipment down the line. "The more gadgets you have, the more opportunity there is for a breakdown," says builder Mark De Mattei. "But if you work with experienced installers, the chances of a problem will decrease significantly."

OPPOSITE PAGE, TOP Putting toiletries on a shower caddy helps them dry more quickly and not allow mold to grow underneath as it might if they sat on the edge of the tub or on the shower floor.

OPPOSITE PAGE, CENTER This polished chrome bath caddy straddles the edge of the bathtub, providing a secure and easy-to-reach place for soap and shampoo.

OPPOSITE PAGE, BOTTOM Clear glass vessels turn soaps, sponges, and bath salts into display pieces.

ABOVE A flat-panel television set into a niche in the wall is perfectly positioned for watching a favorite show during an evening soak.

There are seemingly endless choices in cabinet hardware, but you can narrow them down significantly on the basis of quality. "Hardware can become an underutilized element," warns interior designer Terrell Goeke. "If you buy cheap hardware, it makes the cabinets look cheap. Don't overlook the importance of this decision, as it is a highly visible element that can complete the design," he says.

Websites often have the widest variety of styles, but it's important to touch cabinet hardware and feel its weight, so try to shop for knobs and pulls in person if you can, or order from a site that accepts returns. Look for solid, heavy knobs instead of hollow-back knobs. Also examine the finish. If it looks plasticky or lacquered, move on to the next manufacturer. Then narrow down the list of manufacturers to two or three on the basis of quality and aesthetics.

Choosing cabinet hardware is a matter of personal style. Architect Bill Ingram prefers small, discreet knobs and keyholes, while interior designer Lou Ann Bauer looks at hardware as a way to get color and personality into the bathroom (see pages 200–201). Hardware must also be functional. Knobs and pulls should be easy to grab, have no sharp edges that can scratch you as you walk by, and be sized correctly for the door or drawer you're installing them on. Loose pieces on hardware that you have to lift and pull will eventually bang up the cabinet (unless there's a back plate that the piece hits), so it's best to stay away from those.

INTERIOR DESIGNER
LOU ANN BAUER ON

Choosing Hardware Styles

Choosing knobs and pulls for a bathroom is like choosing the right jewelry for a particular dress. "They can give a custom, exciting look to plain cabinetry or build upon an established style, such as Craftsman hardware on Craftsman cabinets. In my San Francisco cabinet hardware store, Bauerware, people are currently gravitating toward distressed iron and copper."

OPPOSITE PAGE In a nautical-themed bath, cleats typically used to secure thick ropes on a boat are used as cabinet pulls and towel hooks.

ABOVE Crystal knobs reflect light just like the water in the goldfish bowl.

RIGHT Recessed finger pulls allow these bathroom cabinet doors to bypass each other completely.

BELOW Discreet narrow pulls allow the rich wood grain of this frameless vanity to shine.

TOP LEFT Sleek metal pulls reinforce the look of a clothes dresser being used as a vanity. Their shape is echoed in the angular lines of the towel rack and wall-mount faucet.

TOP RIGHT Cobalt blue glass pulls paired with lavender ceramic tiles add color to this bathroom.

BOTTOM LEFT Multicolored square glass knobs match the glass accent tiles on the floor in this kids' bath.

INTERIOR DESIGNER
TERRELL GOEKE ON

Keeping Knobs Straight

Square and rectangular knobs can be difficult because they have a tendency to turn, so you end up with a line of out-of-square knobs. "To solve this problem, I put a lock washer on the back, and it keeps the knob in place. I also use round knobs a lot because it doesn't matter if they turn."

Install two pulls on wide drawers so they are easier to open.

Fanciful Fittings

Light maple cabinets and a white solid-surface counter allow the glass mosaic walls, bright terrazzo floor tiles, and creative accessories to shine.

OPPOSITE PAGE, LEFT This leaning faucet with a top shaped like a teakettle rivals the cabinet pulls for most playful accessory.

OPPOSITE PAGE, RIGHT Clear glass shower doors don't obscure the tiled walls in the tub surround. The same ceramic pulls that adorn the floating vanity are used on this recessed cabinet.

Interior designer Lou Ann Bauer is known for her creative use of color. In this bathroom shared by two young girls, Lou Ann based the color palette on the cartoonish man and woman cabinet pulls that the girls fell in love with.

The tub surround and wall behind the vanity are covered in glass mosaic tiles. Yellowish-green paint covers the other two walls, giving your eyes a rest from the pixilated tile pattern but keeping with the cheerful feel of the room. Bits of blue and green glass also shine from the terrazzo floor tiles. Lou Ann compensated for the small amount of storage space in the floating custom vanity by designing a narrow wall cabinet that hangs above one side of it, and a recessed cabinet that extends 18 inches past the tub.

The Elements

- **Flooring:** Terrazzo tiles with olive and aqua glass pieces; bone-colored grout

- **Walls:** Glass mosaic tiles in green, yellow, and white; white grout

- **Vanity:** Custom frameless floating cabinets in maple; translucent glass panel in wall cabinet

- **Countertop:** Solid-surface white

- **Sink:** Square undermount in vitreous china

- **Sink Faucet:** Single-lever in polished chrome, operated by the thin lever on top

- **Bathtub and Shower:** Cast-iron alcove bath with a tiled front; glass shower doors

- **Toilet:** One-piece, 1.6 gpf, gravity assisted

- **Lighting:** Recessed compact fluorescent can lights and a long wall sconce with a fluorescent tube

- **Finishing Touches:** Whimsical ceramic pulls; tall, narrow mirror with frosted glass sides; polished-chrome towel bars and shower door handle; framed art prints that match the style of the pulls

Upscale Vintage

Next to the corner shower is a padded window seat with extra storage underneath.

OPPOSITE PAGE, LEFT Horizontal bars under the console sinks are used for hanging decorative hand towels. Round brushed-nickel pulls are used on the vanity drawers, cabinets around the window, and medicine cabinets.

OPPOSITE PAGE, RIGHT Double towel bars flank the freestanding tub. An octagonal table provides a handy place to set books and magazines within reaching distance.

This elegant master bathroom is part of a new shingle-style home designed by architect David Gast and his associates, and interior designer Deborah Michie. The walls are wrapped in high tongue-and-groove beadboard wainscot, a design theme used elsewhere in the house. Above the beadboard, pale blue paint leads to a soaring ceiling filled with natural light from the double-hung wooden windows.

David supplied an incredible canvas for the fixtures, fittings, and details that Deborah chose to give the room its style. Black and white marble tiles in a basket-weave pattern provide visual texture for the wide expanses of open floor. An inviting window seat in one corner is outfitted with a cushion that matches the black woven shade above. Wall-hung

medicine cabinets have more of a vintage look than recessed ones, and they work perfectly above marble-topped console sinks. To finish the decor, brushed silver vases filled with red and white flowers add bright color and fragrance, and embroidered black-and-white hand towels hang on towel bars.

The Elements

- **Flooring:** Carrera marble in a basket-weave pattern

- **Walls:** Painted wainscot and walls in blue and white

- **Vanities:** Double consoles with brushed-nickel legs separated by face-frame painted drawers

- **Countertop:** Carrera marble

- **Sinks:** Undermount vitreous china

- **Sink Faucets:** Widespread in brushed nickel

- **Bathtub:** Cast-iron soaking tub; floor-mounted faucet in brushed nickel with handheld showerhead

- **Shower:** Custom with a white ceramic tile surround and tiled marble floor, marble bench, and "rain" showerhead

- **Lighting:** Schoolhouse-style ceiling fixture; wall sconces with frosted glass shades

- **Finishing Touches:** Hexagonal wooden table; brushed-silver flower vases; brushed-nickel double towel bars and hooks; double-hung "prairie style" windows (these have a smaller upper sash); wall-mounted medicine cabinets; black woven shades; upholstered window-seat cushion; brushed-nickel pulls; blue and white bath mats

Chapter 8

Getting It Done

How do you actually pull off a successful bathroom renovation? The most important step is finding talented and experienced professionals, much like the ones we've relied on throughout this book, to help you with whatever parts of the design and construction you require assistance with. We'll go over who can do what for you and how to seal the deal, review the basics on budgeting and scheduling, and give the latest recommendations on making your new bathroom safe for everyone to use.

The color palette and fixtures were kept simple to let the room's architectural details shine.

Minor bathroom remodels that consist of improvements such as new paint, a new sink faucet, updated accessories such as towel racks and mirrors, and a more efficient toilet are well within the abilities of most homeowners. A major bathroom remodel includes removing a good deal of what's currently there and installing new flooring, sinks and faucets, wall treatments and lights, and either refurbishing or replacing an existing tub or shower surround. You may be able to do some of the work yourself if you have the right skills and tools and the time to take on the project. But most homeowners will rely on experts like bathroom designers and general contractors to manage and execute the work. If you plan to either add on to your house to build a new bathroom or significantly change the existing layout, you will most likely need an architect.

While it's tempting to update only the finish materials, a major bathroom remodel is an excellent opportunity to take the room down to the studs and update all plumbing and electrical rough-ins. Your city may not require it, but builder Mark De Mattei says he wouldn't be advising his clients well if he didn't insist on this issue. "It's highly risky to cover up old pipes with new materials and fixtures. If you have a pipe burst down the line, it could ruin your new bathroom."

OPPOSITE PAGE
Adding a full-length window to the bathroom makes you feel like you're showering in the garden.

ABOVE RIGHT
Select an architect whose style matches your own. Architect Bill Ingram designed this bathroom to feel like an extension of the bedroom, with furniture-style cabinets and calming neutral colors.

ARCHITECT
DENNIS FOX ON

Shopping

I always tell my clients at the beginning of the process, 'You've got a lot of work to do!' Even if they hire me to do all the shopping, they are the ones who need to decide on what kind of tile they want, what kind of sink. I want them to be involved in these decisions," Dennis says. He also encourages people to shop early in the planning and design stage and then to stick to those decisions. "If we know what size tiles we're using on a wall, we can lay out the tiles so that the shower valve is right in the center of a large tile, rather than falling on a grout line or to one side of the tile. These kinds of details make a room and can only happen when decisions about materials are made before construction starts."

Hiring Professionals

Depending on the scope of your remodel, you may only need to rely on retail specialists, or you may be in the market for an architect or general contractor. Keep in mind that you don't have to decide between doing all the work on your own and hiring a complete team of experts. You may choose to subcontract the jobs you're the least comfortable with and do the rest yourself.

ARCHITECTS are state-licensed professionals who can create structurally sound and functional designs, produce building plans that you can submit to city planning departments, help you choose materials, negotiate bids from contractors, and supervise the project. While architects can be consulted on major renovations to existing bathrooms, they are invaluable when you are adding a new room to the house or bumping out an existing bath. They will ensure that the addition works with the overall style, layout, and mechanical systems of the home.

GENERAL CONTRACTORS usually specialize in construction, although some have design skills as well. Depending on whether you hire a large firm or an individual, a contractor may do all the construction work himself or herself, or hire subcontractors for specific parts of the job. Contractors can also order supplies and materials for you, secure building permits, and arrange for inspections.

INTERIOR DESIGNERS are experts in selecting a color palette and style that work with the rest of your house, and some can hire and manage contractors to get the work done. You can find an interior designer who specializes in bathrooms through the American Society of Interior Designers (ASID).

BATHROOM DESIGNERS are certified by the National Kitchen & Bath Association (NKBA) to ensure that these professionals know about the latest building materials and techniques. If shopping time is limited, a bathroom designer will be able to quickly suggest fixtures and materials to suit your budget and style. Some bathroom designers can also manage the construction process.

RETAIL SPECIALISTS who work in cabinet shops and home improvement centers may be able to provide all the assistance you need if you're only doing a minor remodel. Some can provide a finished plan that you can submit to the city planning department (if a permit is required) for a small fee, or even for free if you end up purchasing materials from the store.

Permits

Once you've determined the scope of your remodel, take your plans (even if it's just a rough sketch) to your local building department to see if you need a permit. There will be a fee and your property taxes may increase, but doing some types of construction work without a permit is illegal. If you are caught, you may be required to rip out the work and start

In addition to the major finishes like tile and fixtures, you have the right to specify all the materials that professionals use in your bathroom. If you want a low-VOC caulk or Greenguard-certified adhesives, tell your contractor before the project begins.

over. Your homeowner's insurance may be invalidated, and when you eventually sell the house, you may not be able to include the value of your new or remodeled bathroom if you can't show that the work was permitted.

Remember, the building code is there for your safety and the safety of others. City inspectors will make sure that all work is done correctly and to codes, which protects you from shoddy work that you may not have the expertise to detect.

Hiring high-quality, experienced professionals increases the likelihood that you will be happy with the outcome. As with most things, you get what you pay for.

Architects and interior designers will ensure that the bathroom is harmonious with the rest of the house as well as with the landscape. Here, windows in the bath open onto a private side yard with a bright orange tiled wall that acts as eye candy.

Interviewing

Ask friends and relatives for recommendations on whom to hire. If you aren't working with an architect or general contractor and just need to hire a few professionals in the specialty trades, such as plumbers and electricians, be aware that the good ones are often kept busy with recurring work from builders and may be hard to nail down. Your goal is to find a company or person whose work you can trust and who can also be counted on to show up when necessary.

Give the professional an idea of your schedule and budget and ask if the project sounds like something he or she can take on. Depending on the type of professional you're hiring, you may at this point want to schedule a meeting. Architect Beth Gensemer advises looking at pictures of past work to see if a person's aesthetic matches your own. "When architects, designers, or builders show you their work and you see a general consistency in the design, it's safe to assume you'll get the same consistency. But if their work shows a variety of styles, it's safe to assume they might be able to do something different for you," she says.

Ask the professional for at least three recent references and call them. Past clients should be able to tell you if the quality of the professional's work was good, if the crew showed up on time and when scheduled, if the crew kept the area clean and was courteous and respectful of the home, and if the work was completed on time. Also be sure you know whether the professional you interview will be doing the work himself or herself, or if the work will be carried out by an associate or other employees, and if that's the case, see if you can meet those people before making a final decision. Get at least three quotes, and resist the temptation to pick the lowest price. Sometimes a low bid means that the person is new and inexperienced, and other times it may be a way to get you to sign an open-ended contract whereby the price might be increased significantly in the end.

Make sure any building professional is licensed, bonded, and insured. That means that he or she is registered with the state, any legal problems would be paid for, and any damage to your home or injury to an employee working in your home would be covered.

Contracts

Once you've found a person you feel is reputable, who gives a fair price for the work proposed, and whose references have checked out, you can offer that professional the job. If you're hiring an architect, designer, or general contractor for a complete bathroom remodel, you should have a contract that clearly states the job requirements, fee, and schedule. Hire a

Hire an architect or interior designer when you want something unique, such as this master bath with custom rowboat tub, oversized spotlights, and checkerboard mirror.

lawyer to review the contract if you are unsure of the terms. Smaller jobs that last only a few days usually don't require a contract.

Some contractors propose a fixed price, which can cover either labor only or labor and materials. A time and materials contract means you're being charged an hourly rate and materials will be extra. If the professional asks for a down payment, it shouldn't be more than 20 percent of the total job amount, unless you're asking the person to buy materials up front. When someone buys materials for you, always make sure you get a copy of the receipts. Remaining payments should be tied to milestones in the project, or, for very short projects, payment is due when the job is completed to your satisfaction.

Budget and Timing

Interspersing a few dozen glass tiles among less expensive white subway tiles saved the owners of this bathroom a considerable amount of money.

The total cost for your bathroom remodel will depend on many factors, including how extensive the project is, where you live, what types of materials you're using, and whether you're doing any portions of the work yourself. Taking the time to plan your bathroom remodel carefully and then not changing your mind on layout or materials once construction begins will save you money.

You might think that a bathroom remodel wouldn't be that expensive because it's one of the smaller rooms in the house, but builder Mark De Mattei points out that you need the same number of tradespeople working on it as you would when remodeling any other room, including framers, electricians, plumbers, drywallers, and tile setters. Given the number of people coming and going, scheduling is critical.

The pie chart above shows an average breakdown of where your money will be spent. Labor and design can account for approximately 30 percent of the total job amount. If you are confident of your skills to either design your new bathroom or do all or part of the construction, you can save a good deal of money. Be realistic about what you can do, though, or you may end up having to hire someone to fix a problem you created.

You should be able to get a sense of how much money materials will cost during the planning stage. Price materials and fixtures you like and use your base plan (see pages 32–35) to calculate how many square feet of flooring and how many linear feet of cabinets and countertops you will need. There are lots of ways to keep the costs down without sacrificing quality, such as using mass-produced field tiles in a stock color and custom glass tiles as an accent or border (as seen on the opposite page) rather than using expensive glass tiles across the entire wall.

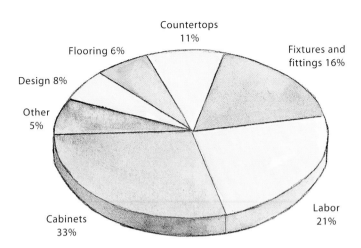

Countertops 11%
Flooring 6%
Design 8%
Other 5%
Fixtures and fittings 16%
Cabinets 33%
Labor 21%

Instead of purchasing a new vanity, find an old bedside table at a flea market and give it a fresh look with paint and new pulls.

Interviewing contractors and designers in your area is the only way to get an accurate sense of their fees. In general, design professionals like architects, bathroom designers, and interior designers often charge about 10 percent of the total cost of the project (including materials) if they are designing the space, hiring contractors, and overseeing the construction. You can also choose to pay an hourly fee just for the design.

Once the project starts, keep it on track by managing it closely, or by hiring someone who will do this for you. Make sure flooring, fixtures, and other materials are ordered in advance of when construction will begin so that contractors aren't waiting for supplies that will hold up progress. Generally, after demolition, the order of work is as follows: structural changes; rough plumbing and electrical; installing the bathtub or shower; wall and ceiling finishes; light fixtures; cabinets and countertops; toilet and sink; flooring; and, finally, finishing touches like window treatments, mirrors, and towel bars.

Universal Design

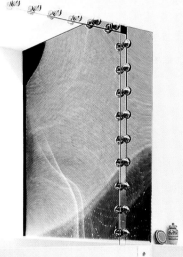

The Americans with Disabilities Act (under the U.S. Department of Justice) publishes the ADA Standards for Accessible Design, which provides standards and clearances needed to accommodate people in wheelchairs. View the latest report at www.ada.gov to get the information you need for your bathroom remodel. Even if everyone in your household is currently young and healthy, it's wise to think ahead and incorporate some of these features.

To make the bathroom user-friendly for a wide variety of people, install nonslip flooring, handheld showerheads, and rocker switches (a flat panel instead of a protruding light switch). Knobs and levers should be operable with one hand without having to be grasped tightly. If you're opening up the walls around the shower, tub, and toilet area, add plywood reinforcement and bracing between the wall studs so that you have something solid to drill into later on if you need to install grab bars.

Choosing Safe Materials

While it's important that the bathroom look and function the way you want it to, safety should be a primary consideration when you're deciding on everything from flooring to accessories.

Choose water-resistant and nonslip flooring in the bathroom, and especially in front of the tub or shower. Bath mats and rugs should have nonskid backing. Towel bars, hooks, and countertops should have rounded edges so they won't cause an injury if you run into them.

Take every precaution to ensure that electrical devices are used safely in the bathroom. If you are pulling a permit for your bathroom remodel, your city will require that all of your electrical receptacles be protected by ground-fault circuit interrupters (GFCIs). Even if you're not doing a major remodel, you should replace any existing receptacles with GFCIs, which will protect you from a bad shock or electrocution by instantly shutting down power to the receptacle if electrical current begins to leak anywhere throughout the circuit.

To prevent accidental scalding, the water heater should be set to 120 degrees or less and scald-free shower and tub valves should be installed (see page 147). Glass mirrors and shower doors should be tempered so they won't shatter if broken.

OPPOSITE PAGE Modern and minimalist, this bathroom can also accommodate a person in a wheelchair with its open, curbless shower, wall-hung sink with hidden plumbing, and motion-sensing faucets.

ABOVE RIGHT Building a seat into the shower is useful both for propping up a leg while shaving and for people with limited strength to sit on.

ARCHITECT
BETH GENSEMER ON

Grab Bars

Many people who aren't disabled may still need grab bars around the toilet and in the tub and shower as they get older and lose a little stability. "If you put bracing in the walls for future grab bars, you might not remember exactly where it is a few years down the line. So if you think you'll need grab bars soon, you might as well put them in during the remodel."

Resources

The following are organizations, manufacturers, and retailers mentioned in this book, along with a variety of others you might find helpful in creating your new bathroom—with an emphasis on companies dedicated to environmentally responsible manufacturing processes and/or products.

Organizations and Planning

ADA Standards for Accessible Design
www.ada.gov

American Institute of Architects
www.aia.org

American Society of Interior Designers
www.asid.org

Forest Stewardship Council
www.fsc.org
Nonprofit organization devoted to encouraging the responsible management of the world's forests

Greywater Systems
www.greywater.com
Reusing water from sinks and showers in the garden

Home Ventilating Institute
www.hvi.org

National Kitchen and Bath Association
www.nkba.org

WaterSense
www.epa.gov/watersense
A program that identifies high-efficiency fixtures

Floors and Walls

AFM Safecoat
www.afmsafecoat.com
Environmentally responsible paints, stains, sealers, and more

Ann Sacks
www.annsacks.com
Tile, stone, and more

Fireclay Tile
www.fireclaytile.com
Handmade tile

Fired Earth
www.firedearth.com
Tiles and more

Granada Tile
www.granadatile.com
Cement and concrete tile

Marmoleum
www.forbo-flooring.com
Linoleum

Roppe
www.roppe.com
Rubber floor tiles and more

Sierra Pine
www.sierrapine.com
Makers of Medite and Medex MDF products

SwitchLite Privacy Glass
www.switchlite.com

Walker Zanger
www.walkerzanger.com
Tiles

Yolo Colorhouse
www.yolocolorhouse.com
Environmentally responsible paint with a natural palette

Countertops

Buddy Rhodes Artisan Concrete
www.buddyrhodes.com

CaesarStone
www.caesarstone.com
Quartz

Corian
www.corian.com
Solid surface

EnviroGLAS
www.enviroglasproducts.com
Recycled glass and porcelain terrazzo

FireSlate
www.fireslate.com
Fiber cement

Formica
www.formica.com
Laminate countertop

IceStone
www.icestoneusa.com
Recycled glass and concrete countertop

PaperStone
www.paperstoneproducts.com
Solid-surface counter made of recycled paper

Richlite
www.richlite.com
Paper-based solid-surface countertop

Sonoma Cast Stone
www.sonomastone.com
Concrete countertops and more

Squak Mountain Stone
www.squakmountainstone.com
Mix of materials made to resemble stone

ThinkGlass
www.thinkglass.com
Glass countertops and more

Trinity Glass
www.trinityglassproducts.com
Glass and concrete countertops

Vetrazzo
www.vetrazzo.com
Recycled glass

Wilsonart
www.wilsonart.com
Solid surface

Cabinets

KraftMaid
www.kraftmaid.com
Semicustom cabinets

Merillat Cabinetry
www.merillat.com
Stock and semicustom cabinets

Neil Kelly
www.neilkellycabinets.com
Semicustom cabinets

Fixtures

Amerec Sauna & Steam
www.amerec.com
Infrared heat room/dry sauna and steam showers

Aquatic Bath
www.aquaticbath.com
Whirlpools, soaking tubs, steam systems, shower doors, and more

Bauerware
www.bauerware.com
Cabinet hardware

Broan-NuTone
www.broan-nutone.com
Ventilation

DCE Bathing Systems
www.serenitytubs.com

Diamond Spas
www.diamondspas.com
Custom metal tubs and more

Duravit
www.duravit.com
Sinks, tubs, and more

Fantech
www.fantech.net
Ventilation fans

The Home Depot
www.homedepot.com

Infinity Drain
www.infinitydrain.com
Linear drain systems

Kohler
www.us.kohler.com
*Sinks, faucets, tubs, toilets,
and accessories*

Lowe's
www.lowes.com

Mr. Steam
www.mrsteam.com
Steambaths and more

Nuheat
www.nuheat.com
Electric floor heat systems

Oceania Baths
www.oceaniabaths.com
Walk-in baths and more

Toto
www.toto.com
*Tubs, toilets, sinks, faucets, and
showerheads*

WS Bath Collections
www.wsbathcollections.com
Wood tubs and more

Lighting

Rejuvenation
www.rejuvenation.com
Lighting, hardware, and accessories

Solatube
www.solatube.com
Daylighting

Credits

We would like to thank the designers, architects, and builders who contributed to this book, and the homeowners who graciously allowed us to photograph their bathrooms.

Photography

ACP/trunkarchive.com: 3 left, 3 right, 67, 107 top, 157, 199, 205, 213, 223; Dave Adams: 54 right; Serge Anton/Living Inside: 11 both, 16 bottom, 18, 44 right, 129 top right, 187, 214; courtesy of APCOR—Portuguese Cork Association: 48, 49 top left; Michel Arnaud/Beateworks/Corbis: 173 bottom right; Scott Atkinson: 159 top middle; Fernando Bengoechea/Beateworks/Corbis: 169; Andrew Bordwin/Beateworks/Corbis: 56 top; Kira Brandt/Pure Public/Living Inside: 170 bottom, 208, 209; Marion Brenner: 13, 42 middle, 119 right, 134 top right, 193; courtesy of Broan-NuTone: 165 both; Rob Brodman: 194 top left, 194 top middle; Rob D. Brodman: 60 top middle, 60 middle right; Sharyn Cairns: 49 top right, 156 top, 162 right; B. Claessens/Inside/Photozest: 101 top left; Comstock/Jupiterimages: 32–33; Jonn Coolidge: 25, 55 both, 80 right, 86, 108 top right, 110, 134 bottom left, 137, 160; courtesy of Corian: 90 left; Carlos Dominguez/Corbis: 173 bottom left; Frederic Ducout/Living Inside: 85, 111 bottom, 143 right, 211; John Dummer/Taverne Agency: 72 bottom right, 108 left; courtesy of Duravit: 103 top left; Hotze Eisma/Taverne Agency: 138; David Fenton: 2 right, 37; courtesy of Fired Earth (photographer: Emma Lee): 40 right, 54 left, 56 bottom, 79 top, 88 middle right; courtesy of Formica Corporation: 45, 82, 83 bottom; Frank Gaglione: inside back cover flap top; William Geddes: 38, 153; William Geddes/

Beateworks/Corbis: 59 right, 87 bottom; Lenora Gim/Botanica/Jupiterimages: 139 bottom; Tria Giovan: 135, 178–179, 198 bottom left, 207; courtesy of Gleen Glass Studios: 109 bottom; Alina Gozina/Taverne Agency: 166 bottom; Jay Graham: 14–15, 70 bottom; Art Gray: 50 left, 72 top left; M. Green/H&L/Inside/Photozest: 75 bottom left, 76 bottom; Margot Hartford: 60 top left, 190; Philip Harvey: 70 top; Tom Haynes: 50 middle top, 50 top right, 50 bottom right, 60 bottom left, 60 bottom right, 61 top; Douglas Hill/Beateworks/Corbis: 43, 75 bottom right, 134 top left, 143 left; courtesy of IceStone: 84 bottom; Image Studios: 170 top; courtesy of Infinity Drain and Easy Drain: 142 right; H&L/Inside/Photozest: 99 top right; InsideOutPix/Jupiterimages: 59 bottom left; Bjarni B. Jacobsen/Pure Public//Living Inside: 12 bottom left; Pernille Kaalund/Pure Public/Living Inside: 19 bottom, 163 right; Rob Karosis: 158; Nicole Katano: 4 top right; Muffy Kibbey: 162 left, 168–169, 198 top right; Jansje Klazinga/Taverne Agency: 128; Robbert Koene/Taverne Agency: 73; courtesy of Kohler: 109 top, 114, 116 top, 127 middle, 136 bottom right, 139 middle, 147; courtesy of Kraftmaid: 71 bottom; Nathalie Krag/Taverne Agency: 29, 75 top, 191 right; K. Krogh/House of Pictures/Inside/Photozest: 77 left; Eva Kylland/Living Inside: 16 top; courtesy of Lasco: 141 bottom; David Duncan Livingston: 78, 79 bottom, 81 left, 99 bottom left, 108 bottom right, 113, 131 bottom, 141 top left, 142 left; David Matheson: front cover (styling: Philippine Scali; props: Ethel Brennan; glass canisters, bath caddy, and bath linens courtesy of Pottery Barn); Ellen McDermott: 98, 100 top, 105, 192 bottom left; E. Andrew McKinney: 46, 141 top right, 159 left, 159 bottom middle, 159 right; Rob Melnychuk/Brand X Pictures/Jupiterimages: 126; courtesy of Merillat Cabinetry: 70

middle, 71 top, 75 middle; Laura Moss: 1, 2 left, 7, 12 top left, 41 right, 51, 53 top, 69, 89, 186 bottom; courtesy of Oceania: 131 middle, 134 bottom right; Alejandro Peral/Living Inside: 154; Sarramon-Cardinale Photononstop/Jupiterimages: 49 bottom left; Photoshot/Lived In: 130 bottom; Photoshot/Red Cover/Nina Assam: 219; Photoshot/Red Cover/Grey Crawford: 101 bottom right, 115 left; Photoshot/Red Cover/Jake Fitzjones: 116 middle; Photoshot/Red Cover/Douglas Gibb: 119 left; Photoshot/Red Cover/Paul-Ryan Goff: 144 bottom, 163 left; Photoshot/Red Cover/Stewart Grant: 12 top right, 47 right, 172 top; Photoshot/Red Cover/Ken Hayden: 107 bottom, 172 bottom; Photoshot/Red Cover/Sarah Hogan: 182; Photoshot/Red Cover/James Kerr: 185 top; Photoshot/Red Cover/Sandra Lane: 104 top; Photoshot/Red Cover/David Duncan Livingston: 129 top left, 131 top, 133, 146; Photoshot/Red Cover/Peter Margonelli: 59 top left; Photoshot/Red Cover/Paul Massey: 173 top left; Photoshot/Red Cover/Simon McBride: 106, 127 bottom; Photoshot/Red Cover/Niall McDiamid: 132 right, 194 top right; Photoshot/Red Cover/Minh & Wass: 125; Photoshot/Red Cover/Keith Scott Morton: 112; Photoshot/Red Cover/Ed Reeve: 181; Photoshot/Red Cover/Evan Sklar: 3 middle, 97; Photoshot/Red Cover/Sue Stubbs: 118 left; Photoshot/Red Cover/Verity Welstead: 136 left; Photoshot/Red Cover/Andrew Wood: 100 bottom; Pure Public/Living Inside: 19 top; Ken Rice: 144 top left, 171; Lisa Romerein: 117, 136 top right, 192 top left, 197 middle, 210; Lisa Romerein/Botanica/Jupiterimages: 194 middle right; M. Roobaert/Inside/Photozest: 44 left; Eric Roth: 9 left, 22–23 all, 39 top, 39 middle, 40 left, 41 left, 49 bottom right, 57, 58, 60 top right, 64, 65 both, 72 top right, 72 bottom left, 77 bottom left, 77 bottom right, 80 left, 87 top left, 88 left, 90 top right, 99 top left, 101 bottom left, 102, 111 middle, 118 right, 166 top, 167, 173 top right, 189; Prue

Ruscoe/Taverne Agency: 140, 191 left, 206; E. Saillet/Inside/Photozest: 88 top right, 129 bottom left, 145 right; Brian Sanderson/Granada Tile: 42 top; Annie Schlechter: 197 bottom; Susan Seubert: 144 top right; Alan Shortall/Corner House Stock Photo: 77 top right; courtesy of Sonoma Cast Stone: 103 top right, 103 bottom left; courtesy of Squak Mountain Stone: 81 right, 91; Thomas J. Story: 26, 27 top, 56 middle, 155, 194 bottom right, 212, 217; Tim Street-Porter: 9 bottom right, 27 top, 28 bottom, 103 bottom right, 132 left, 185 bottom; courtesy of Toto: 115 right, 116 bottom; Dana van Leeuwen/Taverne Agency: 192 bottom right; Mikkel Vang/Taverne Agency: 161; Dominique Vorillon: 15 all, 16–17, 24 all, 28 top, 62–63, 74, 99 bottom right, 111 top, 130 top, 139 top, 145 left, 164, 184, 198 top left; courtesy of Walker Zanger: 88 bottom right; Bjorn Wallander: 10, 188; Julian Wass: 30–31, 52, 84 top, 87 top right, 129 bottom right, 183, 195, 215; Wendell Webber/Botanica/Jupiterimages: 76 top; Michele Lee Willson: 8, 9 top right, 12 bottom right, 20–21 all, 35 top, 39 bottom, 42 bottom, 47 left, 68, 83 top, 92, 93 both, 94, 95 both, 101 top right, 120, 121, 122–123 all, 127 top, 148–149 all, 150–151 all, 174–175 both, 176–177 all, 196, 197 top, 200–201 all, 202–203 all; courtesy of Wilsonart: 90 bottom right; Polly Wreford/navalisimages.com: 61 bottom; Hans Zeegers/Taverne Agency: 53 bottom, 104 bottom, 156 bottom, 186 top left, 186 top right

Design

2 left: Frank DelleDonne; 7: Frank DelleDonne; 8: Kathryn Rogers, Sogno Design Group; 9 left: Horst Buchanan Architects, www.horstbuchanan.com; 9 top right: Anne Laird-Blanton, architect; 12 top left: Elaine and Jim Alt; 12 bottom right: built by Behrens Curry, interior design by Regina Interiors; 13: Boor Bridges Architecture; 14–15: Cillesa N. Ullman, Calahan Design Group; 16–17: Carol Tink Fox, architect; 20 top:

David Gast & Associates Architects, Pete Retondo at RCI Construction, Deborah Michie Interior Design, Amy DeVault Interior Design; **20–21 crossover, 21 both:** Kathryn Rogers, Sogno Design Group; **23 bottom:** S&H Construction, www.shconstruction.com; **24 all:** Judi Naftulin; **27 top:** Bernie Baker Architects; **27 bottom:** Kelly Harmon; **28 top:** Beth Gensemer; **28 bottom:** Alice Kimm; **30–31:** Hein + Cozzi, Inc.; **35 top:** David Gast & Associates Architects, Pete Retondo at RCI Construction, Deborah Michie Interior Design, Amy DeVault Interior Design; **38:** Gerry Williams, prop stylist; **39 top:** Stern McCafferty Architect & Design; **39 middle:** Trikeenan Tileworks; **40 left:** Salt Water Design Group; **40 right:** tiles from Fired Earth, www.firedearth.com; **41 left:** www.fbnconstruction.net; **41 right:** Nancy Jeffrey Studio 211 Ltd; **42 top:** cement tiles by Granada Tile, interior design by Mission Tile West; **42 middle:** Lindy Small Architecture; **43:** Larry Bogdanow, architect; design by Daniel Sachs & Fernando Santangelo; **46:** Debra S. Weiss and D. Kimberly Smith, Deer Creek Design; **49 bottom left:** Heidi Pribell Interior Design; **52:** Jeffrey Bilhuber; **53 top:** New World Home, builder; **54 left:** tiles from Fired Earth, www.firedearth.com; **54 right:** Reynolds Gualco Architecture-Interior Design, interior design by Robin Hardy Design, construction by Thomas Irvin; **56 top:** Robin Upchurch; **56 bottom:** tiles from Fired Earth, www.firedearth.com; **57:** Heidi Pribell Interior Design; **58:** Space Craft Architecture; **59 right:** Sterling Baths; **60 top left:** David S. Gast & Associates Architects; interior design by Kathy Geissler Best at KGB Associates, construction by Plath & Co. Inc., lighting by Anna Victoria Koldoff; **60 top middle:** tiles from Fireclay Tile; **60 middle right:** wallpaper by Cavern, www.cavernhome.com; **62–63:** Beth Wells Gensemer, Architect; **64, 65 both:** Heidi Pribell Interior Design; **68:** Behrens Curry Inc.,

builders; interior design by Regina Interiors; **69:** Rachel Reider; **70 bottom:** Jane Ellison Design; **72 top right:** Pappas Miron Interior Design; **72 bottom left:** Dressing Rooms; **74:** Madeline Stuart; **75 bottom right:** design and archicture by Freya Block; **79 top:** tiles from Fired Earth, www.firedearth.com; **80 left:** Space Craft Architecture; **83 top:** Anne Laird-Blanton; **84 top:** Marmol Radziner; **87 top left:** Gregor Cann Design; **87 top right:** Shawn Henderson Interior Design; **87 bottom:** Sterling Baths; **88 left:** Tricia McDonagh Interior Design; **88 top right:** decoration by Dovy Elmalan; **88 middle right:** tiles from Fired Earth, www.firedearth.com; **88 bottom right:** tiles from Walker Zanger; **89:** Jamie Herzlinger Interiors; **90 top right:** Design Elements Interior Design; **92–93 all:** Kathryn Rogers, Sogno Design Group; **94–95 all:** David Gast & Associates Architects, Jessica Allee; **99 bottom right:** G. Irani; **101 top left:** decoration by Luc & Sandra Baetens; **101 top right:** J.P. Lindstrom Inc., builder; design by Residential Design; **101 bottom left:** Terrat Elms Interior Design; **102:** Gayle Mandle Design; **103 bottom right:** Steve Hermann; **105:** Lynn Byrne; **111 middle:** fixtures by Ferguson/JD Daddario, tile by TileShowcase; **117:** Helene Aumont; **118 right:** Heidi Pribell Interior Design; **119 right:** Stanley Saitowitz; **120–123 all:** Fox Design Group and David Deveau, Deveau Construction; **129 bottom left:** decoration by Dovy Elmalan; **129 bottom right:** Peter Mark & Elizabeth Needham; **132 left:** Joseph Giovannini; **134 top left:** Alexander, architect; design by Mark Nichols & Dan Wright; **134 top right:** Joseph Bellom, Bellomo Architects; **136 left:** Rebecca Partridge; **136 top right:** Sue Glasscock; **139 top:** Marcus Mohon, architect; **141 top right:** Christine E. Barnes; **143 left:** West Park Interiors; **144 top left:** Kathryn Rogers, Sogno Design Group; **144 top right:** Adam Christie/Prototype Architecture; **145 right:** Bernard Mazerat, architect; **148–149 all:** Kathryn Rogers,

Sogno Design Group; **150–151 all:** De Mattei Construction; **153:** Gerry Williams, prop stylist; **155:** Susan Hornbeak-Ortiz; **158:** Robert Cain, architect; **162 left:** Philip Volkmann/Barry & Volkmann; **163 right:** styling by Louise Kamman Riising; **164:** Martha Angus; **166 top:** Thomas Buckborough & Associates, www.tbadesigns.com; **167:** Horst Buchanan Architects, www.horstbuchanan.com; **168–169:** Philip Volkmann/Barry & Volkmann; **171:** Kathryn Rogers, Sogno Design Group; **173 top right:** Butz & Klug, www.bkarch.com; **173 bottom right:** Michael Formica Inc.; **174–177:** Anne Laird-Blanton, architect; **178–179:** Bill Ingram, architect; interior design by Mary Evelyn McKee; **184:** Denise Domergue; **185 bottom:** Stephen Kanner; **186 bottom:** Jamie Herzlinger Interiors; **188:** art direction by Philippine Scali, styling by Ethel Brennan, fabric for shades from Hable Construction (www.hableconstruction.com); **190:** David S. Gast & Associates Architects, interior design by Kathy Geissler Best at KGB Associates, construction by Plath & Co., lighting by Anna Victoria Koldoff; **192 top left:** Kathryn & David Allen; **192 bottom left:** Kathryn Scott; **193:** Flora Grubb

Gardens; **194 top left:** soap dish from Watson Kennedy Fine Home; **194 top middle:** toothbrushes and holder from Waterworks; **195:** Laura Kirar & Richard Frazier; **196:** David Gast & Associates Architects, Pete Retondo of RCI Construction, Deborah Michie Interior Design, Amy DeVault Interior Design; **197 top:** Behrens Curry, Inc., builders; interior design by Regina Interiors; **197 bottom:** Robert Kaner; **198 top right:** E. Paul Kelly, architect; interior design by Marcy Voyevod Interior Design, cabinets by RK Designs, McCutcheon Construction, Inc.; **200–201 all:** Lou Ann Bauer; **202–203 all:** David Gast & Associates Architects, Pete Retondo of RCI Construction, interior design by Deborah Michie; **207:** Bill Ingram; **210:** Julie Hart; **212:** Ren Chandler of Dyna Contracting; **217:** John Lum Architecture

Illustration

All illustrations by Beverly Bozarth Colgan

Special Thanks

Mark Hawkins,Stephanie Johnson, Charla Lawhon, Marisa Park, Marie Pence, Alan Phinney, Katie Tamony

Index

Sunset guides you to a fabulous home—inside and out

Sunset's all-new Design Guides have everything you need to plan—and create—the home of your dreams. Each book includes advice from top professionals and hundreds of illustrative photos. With an emphasis on green building materials and techniques, this entire series will inspire ideas both inside and outside of your home.

Pull-Out Poster Book

SCHOLASTIC INC.

New York Toronto London Auckland Sydney

ISBN 0-590-06655-2

12 11 10 9 8 7 6 5 4 3 2 1   7 8 9/9 0 1 2/0

Designed by Joan Ferrigno

Printed in the U.S.A.   08

First Scholastic printing, February 1997

R2-D2 and C-3PO: Rebel droids with a secret message.

Luke Skywalker begins his Jedi adventure.

Princess Leia begs Obi-Wan Kenobi for help in defeating the Empire.

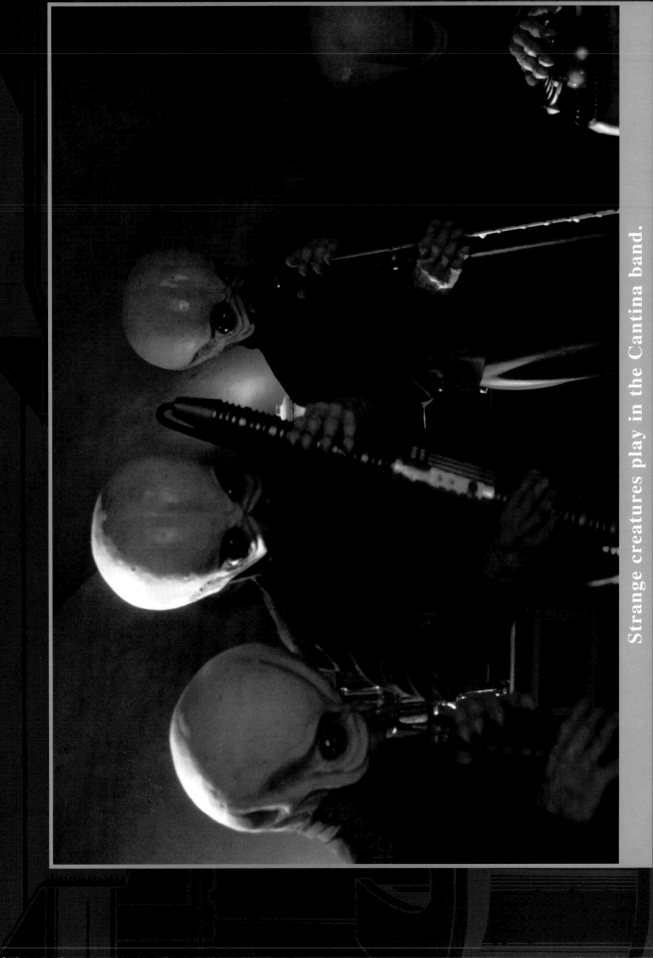

Strange creatures play in the Cantina band.

Han Solo faces off with the villainous Jabba the Hutt.

Han Solo prepares the *Millennium Falcon* for the jump to hyperspace.

Princess Leia watches as the Death Star destroys her planet.

C-3PO suggests a new strategy to R2-D2: letting the Wookiee win.

"There's something alive in here!" screams Luke Skywalker.

Luke Skywalker, Princess Leia, and Han Solo: defenders of the Rebel Alliance.

Stormtroopers chase Luke and Leia through the Death Star.

"I've been waiting for you, Obi-Wan."

Han Solo and Chewbacca — ready for action!

Luke Skywalker boards his X-wing fighter — to destroy the Death Star!

Victory for the Rebel Alliance!